D1824688

CASE STUDIES FOR PRACTICE 1

Day Services for People with Mental Handicaps

2nd edition

Case Studies for Practice

Edited by Philip Seed

Day Services for People with Severe Handicaps
Compiled by Philip Seed
ISBN 1 85302 013 3
Case Studies for Practice 2

Towards Independent Living
Issues for Different Client Groups
Philip Seed and Barbara Montgomery
ISBN 1 85302 018 4
Case Studies for Practice 3

HIV and AIDS: A Social Network Approach
Compiled by Roger Gaitley and edited by Philip Seed
ISBN 1 85302 025 7
Case Studies for Practice 4

Victims of Confusion
Case Studies of Elderly Sufferers from Confusion and Dementia
Alyson Leslie
ISBN 1 85302 040 0
Case Studies for Practice 5

Social Work in the Wake of Disasters
Edited by David Tumelty
ISBN 1 85302 060 5
Case Studies for Practice 6

Respite - A Social Network Approach
Edited by Philip Seed
ISBN 1 85302 061 3
Case Studies for Practice 7

CASE STUDIES FOR PRACTICE 1

Day Services for People with Mental Handicaps 2nd edition

Case material provided by Margaret Thomson and Fiona Pilkington and compiled by Philip Seed

Jessica Kingsley Publishers
London

Editor: Philip Seed
Consultants: Mike King (Social Care Association and Lecturer in Social Work)
                   Ruth Smith (British Association of Social Workers)
                   Fiona Pilkington (Teacher and ex-Researcher)
                   Margaret Thomson (Researcher, Children's Panel Member,
                        Representative for the Rowntree Family Fund and Chairperson
                        of Inverness Committee, L'Arche)
                   David Mitchell (Social Work Education Adviser, Central
                        Council for Education & Training in Social Work,
                        Edinburgh Office)

This edition first published in 1989 by
Jessica Kingsley Publishers Ltd
13 Brunswick Centre
London WC1N 1AF

Printed in Great Britain by
Antony Rowe Ltd, Chippenham, Wiltshire

British Library Cataloguing in Publication Data
Thomson, Margaret, *1936-*
    Day services for people with mental handicaps - 2nd
    ed. - (Case studies for practice; 1)
    1. Mentally handicapped persons. Day care
    I. Title II. Seed, Philip III. Pilkington, Fiona
    IV. Series
    362.3'83

    ISBN .i.1-85302-039-7
    ISSN 0955-7989

CONTENTS

Social network analysis

The case material in this series is based on social network analysis. During the past decade social workers and others in the helping professions have stressed the importance of understanding social networks. For example, it is important to recognise the importance of informal care as well as formal services.

Social network analysis is a new method of systematically measuring social networks. Part of this method consists in asking clients to keep diaries for a monitored period, usually a fortnight. Some months later the exercise is repeated. The diaries are focused on finding out the people, places and activities that are important to clients in daily living. Services are then evaluated in this context. Other 'information components', as they are called, include details of the client's social setting, the client's views and the views of the client's main support person at home (e.g. parent in the case of a child, son or daughter, perhaps, in the case of an elderly person) and assessments of the client's features of performance and interests.

Social network analysis is useful in research, for management and for monitoring services, as well as for individual practitioners. Its research applications are outlined in *Applied Social Network Analysis* (Costello, 1987). Its use for practitioners is described in a forthcoming book *Introducing Network Analysis in Social Work* (Jessica Kingsley, 1989). Dr Philip Seed is the author of both books.

Introduction

Case Studies for Practice presents case material, drawn from research, to illuminate current practice and policy issues in social work. Additionally, some material is compiled specifically for the series.

The idea arose within the Department of Social Work at the University of Aberdeen when researchers became aware that much of the material they gathered was wasted in terms of its illuminative potential for staff training. This especially applied to an evaluative study of day services conducted between 1984 and 1986.*

During this research, 146 individuals and families were closely studied with reference to how the social services in general, and day care services in particular, contributed to their daily lives as a whole.

The first number of _Case Studies for Practice_ was drawn from this research and was entitled _Day Services for People with Mental Handicaps_. It sold out and this second edition contains the original contents together with an additional chapter on day services in rural areas. The additional cases studied also come from the original research but contact has been renewed with the families concerned in order to update developments. We have, therefore, the advantage of what is in effect a longitudinal study from 1984 to 1989.

The case studies are presented in pairs or groups to illustrate particular topics. Firstly we consider two people with mental handicaps who left long-stay hospitals five years ago. What has happened since? How have the social services contributed to their success? - for both of them can be regarded as 'successful' examples of care in the com-

---

* Seed, P., _Day Care at the Crossroads_, Costello, 1988

munity. We then move on to discuss material relating to elderly handicapped people and their even older carers at home. This is a topic so far largely neglected in the literature. Yet it must be of increasing concern to social work managers and practitioners in the future. Next we discuss why some people who are, apparently, very mildly handicapped, come to be placed long-term in day centres. What is their role within the centre? Are they exploited in helping less able clients? What are the implications? Have they become institutionalised within a day care setting, even though they are living at home in the community? These, too, are important topics for the future as we consider changes currently taking place in day care policy and practice. The final chapter considers different approaches to delivering services to clients in remote and rural areas. One idea, for example, is for a peripatetic instructor to visit from the centre to a particular village.

The material is intended for students, especially those on CSS and CQSW courses, in-service training for residential and day care staff, and for all those - including fieldworkers and managers - concerned with the provision of better services. The volume may also be suitable for discussion groups with parents of adults with a mental handicap.

Although names are fictitious, and some specific details may have been slightly altered to avoid identification, the material is authentic and it is our practice to obtain permission from the clients. This permission, we find, is readily given and we are grateful to them for the work that they have put in in keeping diaries and in assisting us in other ways.

Case Studies for Practice can, in some ways, be regarded as a companion series to *Research Highlights* which was also initiated at Aberdeen University, Social Work Department.* *Research Highlights* is designed to summarise research findings for policy makers and practitioners. *Case Studies for Practice* presents issues raised in research or practice studies in terms of individual clients.

---

* *Research Highlights* is also published by Jessica Kingsley

Chapter one

What happened after they left hospital?

Walter and Carol were amongst a group of long-stay residents who left hospital five years ago. They moved first to staffed houses within a special 'village' run by a voluntary society. This rather unusual setting had previously been a well-known children's village. With the reductions of the numbers of children coming into care, it had changed and diversified. Providing stepping stones for adults with mental handicaps leaving hospital was one of its new functions.

It is not clear how much preparation Walter and Carol had had before they left hospital. I was not involved in their lives at that time. But from what they told me it seems to have been rather cursory. They said they were informed one day they had been selected for the move and were then given some training, lasting for a few weeks, to help them to be more independent. My involvement started two years after they had left hospital and they were followed through for a further two years, during which time they moved on from this ex-children's village - Carol to live in a hostel and Walter to live with his friend Susan in a council house in a town about fifteen miles away.

Bearing in mind the hair-raising accounts that one hears of long-stay ex-hospital patients being dumped on their own in the community these must be examples of good practice in terms of community support. But what exactly does community support mean? It is sometimes argued that a step-by-step approach of moving from hospital to hostel, hostel to group home and group home finally to having one's own apartment or house is unsatisfactory. The move from hospital to hostel has been called 'trans-institutionalisation'. Does the evidence of what happened to Walter and Carol justify such statements?

To answer these two main questions, we need to look at the daily living patterns of Walter and Carol over a period of time and assess the restrictions, the opportunities and the support they received from whatever source it came.

Walter

Let us take Walter first. Walter was in the age group 25-30 when he left hospital. He was relatively capable. He could undertake all of what we call self-management skills - for example, dressing, washing, eating and so on - without any assistance or support. He could also perform all of our listed daily living skills except for one; namely, he needed some assistance in understanding money. But this did not inhibit him from going to shops. It was only suggested to us that he relied on the goodwill of shop keepers not to short-change him.

Neither we nor Walter know much about his past. He had been in care since he was a baby and moved to a long-stay hospital when he grew up. It would seem fair to say that this would not happen today and that Walter represents the legacy of mistaken policies in the past.

By the time we met Walter in 1984 he had moved from the staffed house to an associated cottage just outside the village. He shared this cottage with another ex-hospital patient called Susan. By this time Walter had attended an adult training centre for two years. He had, however, been referred from the ATC to a new special project which is also well-known and which offers an alternative kind of day care provision. Walter told us that he attended this special project to help him get out of the ATC and to help him to find a job. The move was highly successful and by the time we met Walter he had just started full time work as a gardener in the grounds of an old people's home.

Figure one shows the network drawing representing fourteen days in Walter's life at this stage. It is based, so far as his home life is con-

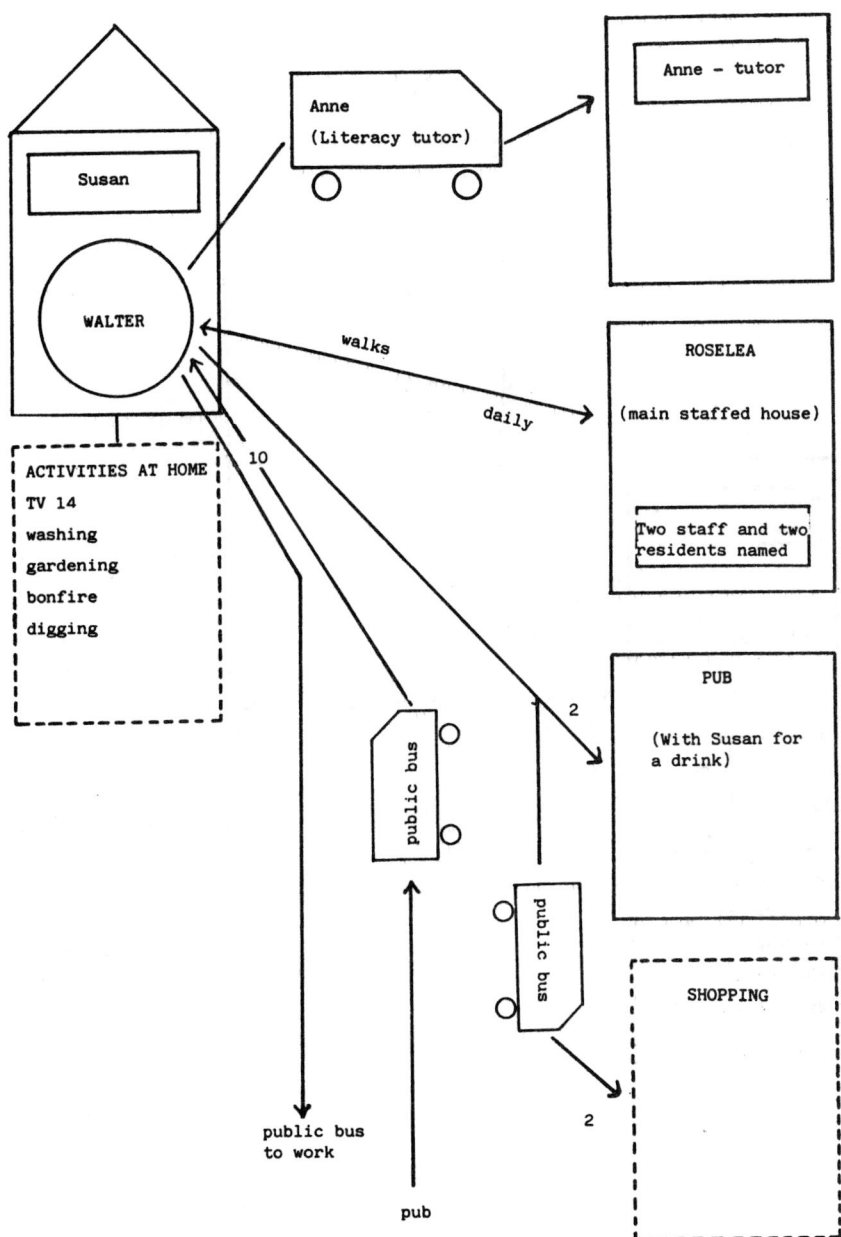

Fig. 1a - Walter, First Monitored Fortnight (Home-based)

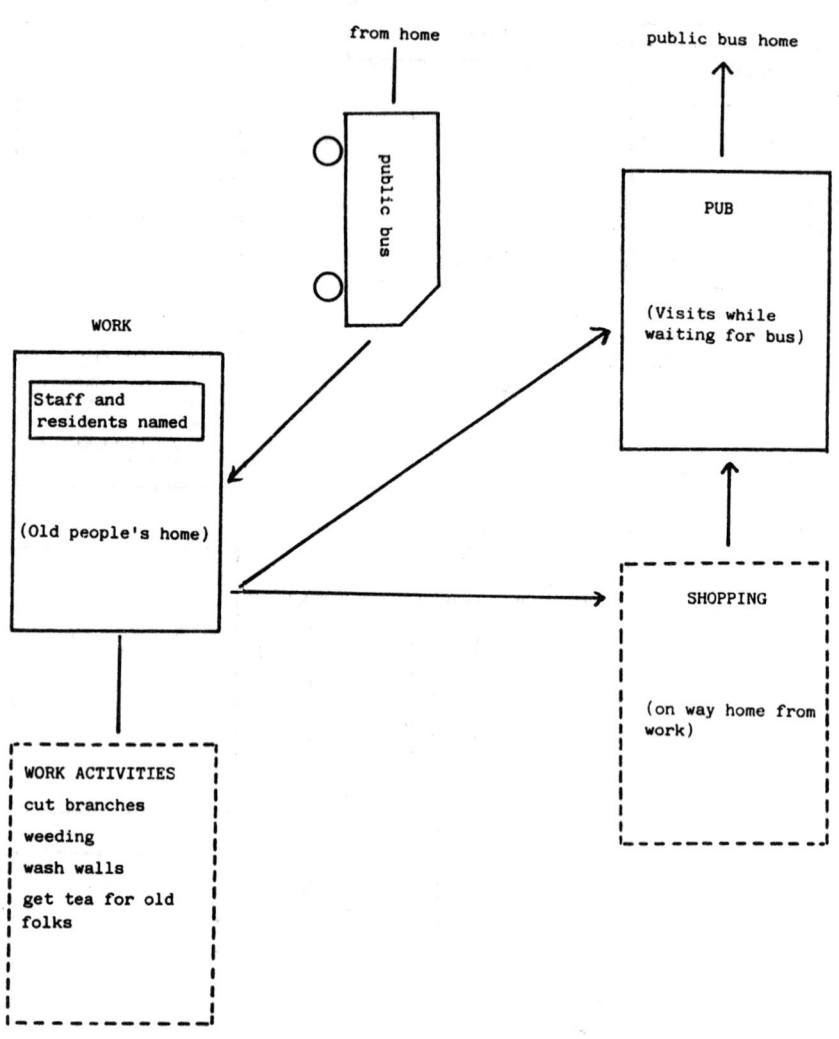

Fig. 1b - Walter, First Monitored Fortnight (Work-based)

cerned, on diaries dictated by him to his key worker in the village. The record of activities at work is based on work sheets completed by him for the day project staff. Perhaps two things stand out from this network. The first is that Walter has friends and the second is that he has initiative in normalising - if I can turn the noun into a verb - his own life. Notice that on the way home from work he goes shopping or visits the pub before catching the country bus to the village. While he has a network of friends within the village he also goes out with his friend Susan from the village. He also takes the bus at the weekend to another town to go shopping. At work he has contact not only with other staff but with some of the residents in the old folk's home. All of this may not seem too surprising except that there is one important point I have not yet mentioned. This is that Walter, apart from having a mild mental handicap, had a stammer which at times could appear to be a severe disadvantage. In talking with him one is immediately impressed by his determination in overcoming it and in not allowing it to prevent him from doing anything he wants to do. We can also see from the network drawing that he is receiving personal adult literacy tuition. He is progressing well. Curiously, though, he is not receiving speech therapy and this was a point that was mentioned to us by his key worker.

I next visited Walter about ten months later. He now lived in a council house, still with Susan and with a third person with a mental handicap who had not come from hospital but who had been encouraged to leave his home and parents. This third person in the group was not present and Walter and Susan explained to me that he did not always fit in so easily, partly because he had his mother on the doorstep. But Walter and Susan remained close friends. They took it in turns to do household chores and share ideas for looking after the place including, for example, starting to do the garden.

This was an ordinary tenancy. They paid their rent monthly. I was told about regular practical help and support that was given by the Social Work Department's Supported Accommodation Team. The project worker was prepared to do such practical things as demonstrate

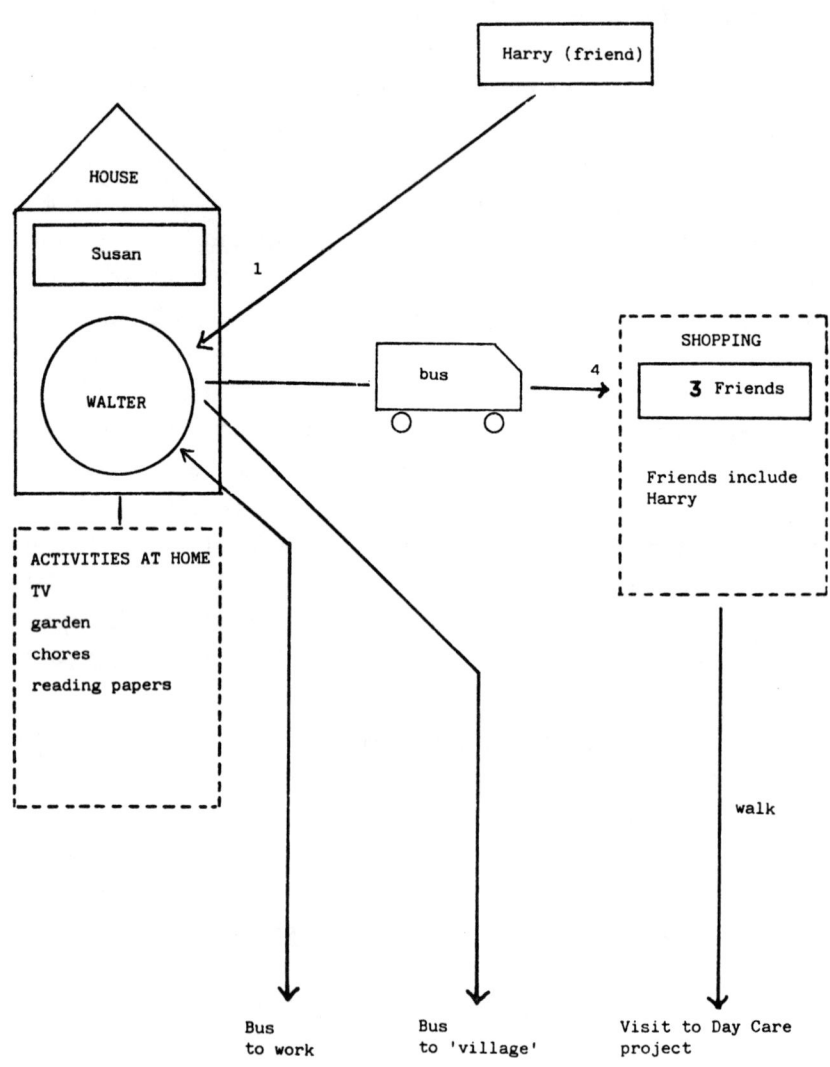

Fig. 2a - Walter, Second Monitored Fortnight (Home-based)

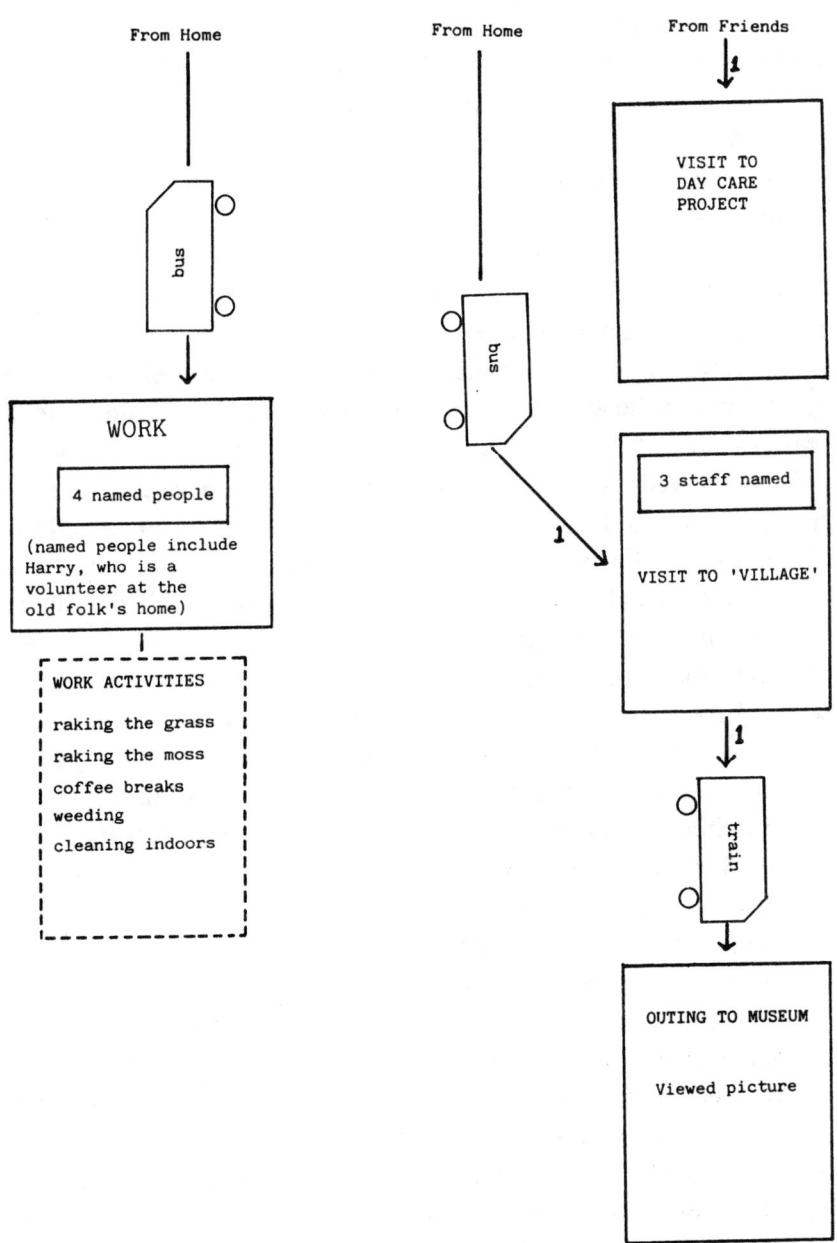

Fig. 2b - Walter, Second Monitored Fortnight (Work-based)

cooking and take them (on the first occasion) to the housing office so that they would know where it was that they had to pay the rent.

I asked Walter what worries or anxieties he had had. He mentioned three main worries. The first was how he would manage money. The second was how he would be able to cook and the third was how he would get on with the neighbours and whether he would feel isolated. He explained that the social worker had helped with the first two of these problems and that the neighbours had turned out to be quite friendly. One had offered to be of assistance if needed. In general, however, Walter explained that the neighbours kept themselves to themselves and that he and Susan did the same. Meanwhile Walter said he was still having his literacy tuition and still working at the same job. He said he enjoyed the summer more than the winter because there was less work to do in the winter time and he got bored. The house and garden were tidy and Walter showed me some of the house painting he had been doing. His stammering seemed much better. He told me he had been offered, or rather asked, if he wanted the services of a speech therapist and he had declined. He said he feared it could make him worse. I asked how he was coming on with his reading and whether he had reached the stage where he could say he enjoyed reading. He said he reads newspapers but his main hobby at home is listening to tapes and watching TV, apart from the gardening. I noticed that the house had a call box telephone. I twice needed 10p change to use it myself and Walter had no difficulty in understanding that $2 \times 5p = 10p$. In general he seemed very relaxed. At one stage he told me some more details about his past that he had found out for the first time. This is not the only case I have come across where people have only been able to find out about their origins after they have left long-stay institutions.

My final visit to Walter was after another six months when we again asked him to keep diaries for us. This time Susan helped him write the diary entries. The network drawing for a fortnight is shown in *figure two*. The third person who shared the tenancy had now left and returned to his parents. He did not fit in and the move was premature, or perhaps he was wrongly placed. Work is going well and we can see that Walter is still in touch with the day care project through which he first obtained the job. Notice that he travels by bus and train - in fact quite long distances - to meet friends and to go on outings. Notice also that one friend visits Walter at home. The house is situated on the very edge of town and this might be off-putting for some people to visit - although a bus takes you right to the door.

In terms of the principles of normalisation, Walter has surely made it.

What was this special day project which did so much for him? The following are some of its key features which distinguish it from a traditional adult training centre. First it has a group intake. Walter was one of eight who started at the same time. On the first day they meet together and mutual support is encouraged.

Secondly they are accorded the status of potential 'workers' from the moment they arrive. Responsibilities for managing the group are shared - responsibilities which vary from who makes the tea to what they are going to do next.

Thirdly, goals are set on the assumption that they will be realised within a limited time span. Unlike a further education college course the time span is not precisely defined in advance but it is assumed to be about a year. The original object - successful in the case of Walter - was to find a job. In an area of over thirty percent unemployment this is not easy and the goal has now been modified to include other forms of community activity.

Fourthly, the centre is not a building, let alone a purpose-built one, where people attend regularly to undertake activities which are fixed from day-to-day, week-to-week or year-to-year. The centre is a resource and those who attend go out to learn the skills they need in the community itself. Before finding work Walter had a series of placement experiences. Some of these could be within the same building since other things, such as an old people's club, were going on in the building. Here are some of Walter's comments at that time:

The centre helps. If you've got any fault you can get over them. If you're stuck with anything you can get help. The day trips were useful. I learnt to travel back and forth. I had to learn numbers. But first I felt helpless.

Walter also received help from a very good key worker from the hostel he first attended and with whom he still maintains contact. He also had exceptional help from an adult literacy tutor. Finally he had received regular help, week by week, from the Supported Accommodation Team of the Social Work Department. This team included a home maker as well as a social worker and there were regular group discussions at the social work office as well as home visits. The team had a wide remit which included both practical help and counselling. They explained to me what would be involved in offering community support, emphasising that it had to be long-term and continuous. It would include, for example:

- helping to develop community awareness

- explaining simple things like how to read maps

- the use of money and making ends meet on a week-to-week basis

- help in making decisions, and solving specific problems in daily living

- getting to know people like neighbours and others

- developing communication skills as well as practical aspects of home and house management including safety.

Granted all this support, Walter had learnt to do many things which at one time he could not do.

All of these forms of help were components of successful care in the community, each of which was indispensable. Linked with this, resources and opportunities were available at the right time. Walter was able to get the tenancy of a house when he needed it. Finally he was allowed to choose, for example, not to have a speech therapist, and his status as an adult was respected.

Carol

Carol was about the same age as Walter and she left a long-stay hospital for patients with mental handicaps at about the same time. Carol is also reasonably capable. She can look after herself in terms of 'self-management' and her performance of most necessary daily living tasks is reasonable. However, when I first met her, she needed a little more support than Walter did, not only in managing money but in getting out and about, especially on public transport.

Carol knew slightly more about her past than Walter did about his. Like Walter, however, more facts were to emerge once she left hospital. As a child she attended ordinary schools and after leaving school had for a time a job in a hotel. It seems that the occasion for her being admitted to a long-stay mental handicap hospital was because she gave birth to a child. The child was subsequently adopted. She showed me a picture of the baby which was amongst her very few personal belongings. Again, as with Walter, can we say that these kind of things would not happen today? It is worth recalling that we are talking about events some fifteen-twenty years ago. It is not a very long time ago.

Carol did not progress so far along the tier system of moves to more independent forms of living within the sheltered village as Walter did. During the first monitored fortnight (*figure three*) she had her own room, with a key to it, within a house. The house was not permanently staffed but staff were available to call as required from a main unit a few hundred yards away on a kind of core and cluster arrangement. The house was within the grounds of the village. Carol was only responsible for cooking snacks - although cooking was one of the things she was good at. Meals were supplied from the main building. It will be seen that she has an active social life within the village community and she

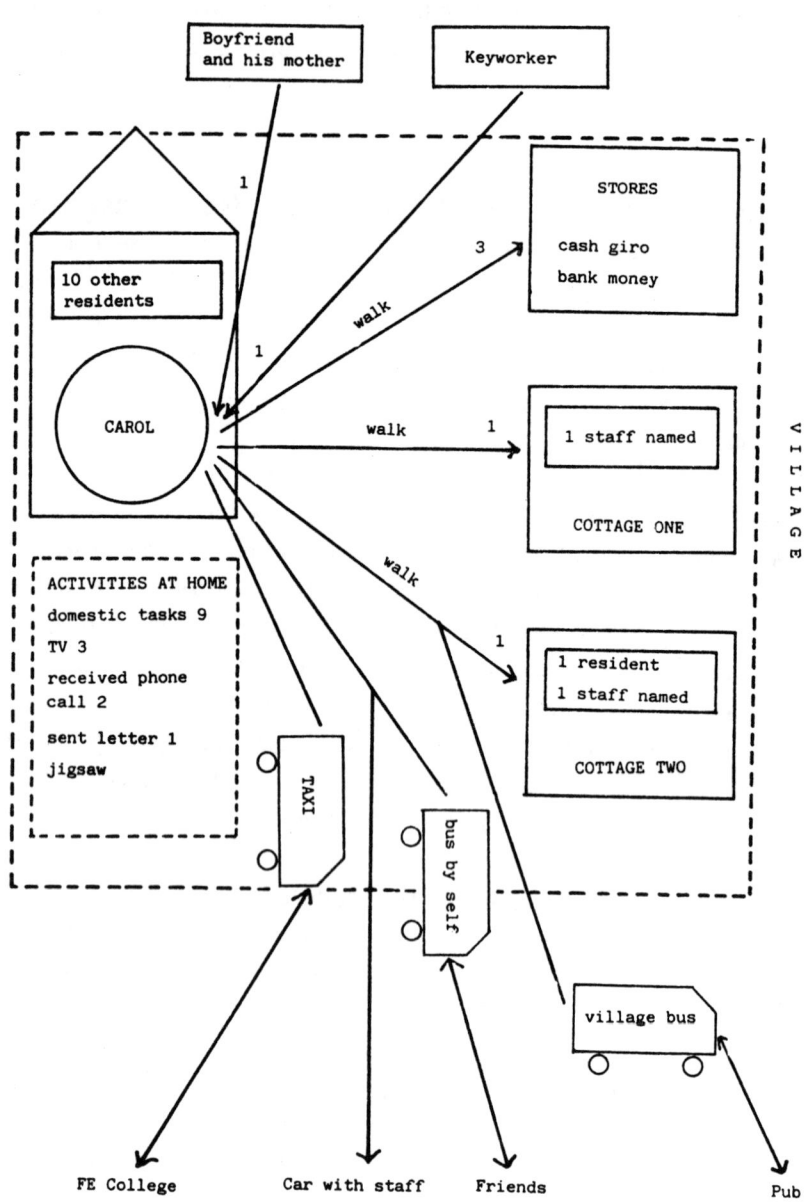

Fig. 3a - Carol, First Monitored Fortnight (within Village)

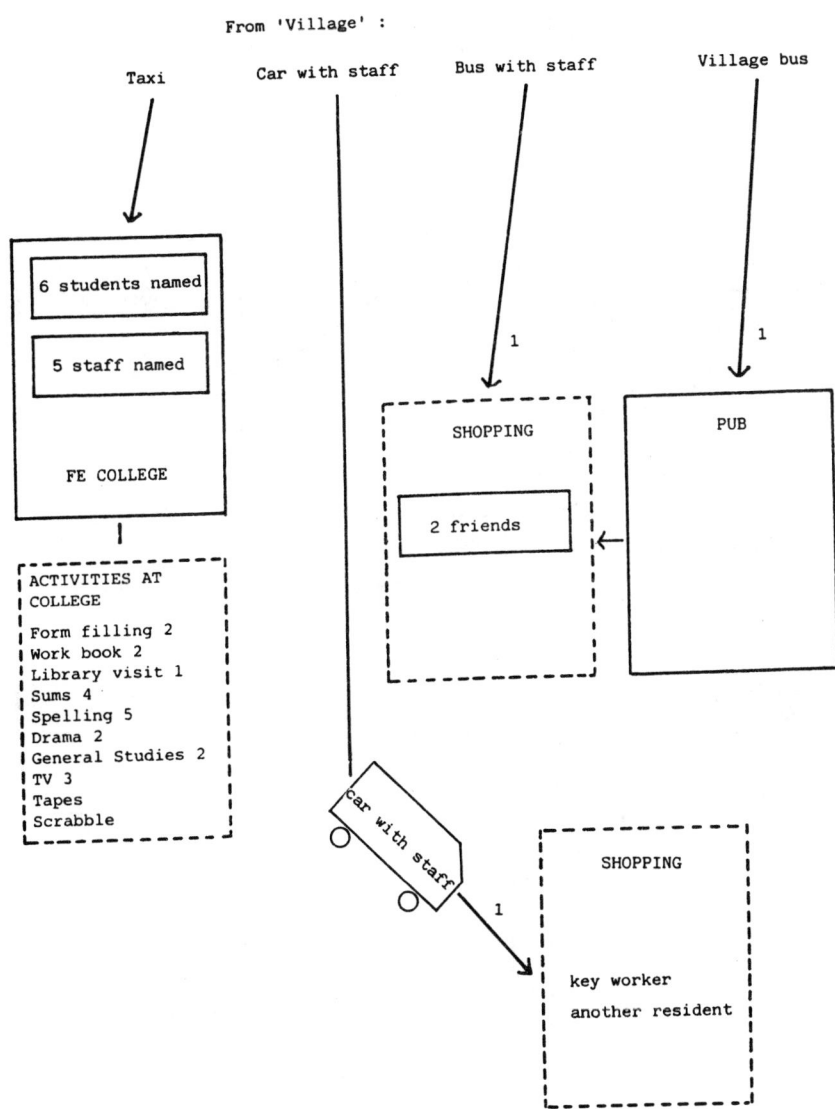

Fig. 3b - Carol, First Monitored Fortnight (outside Village)

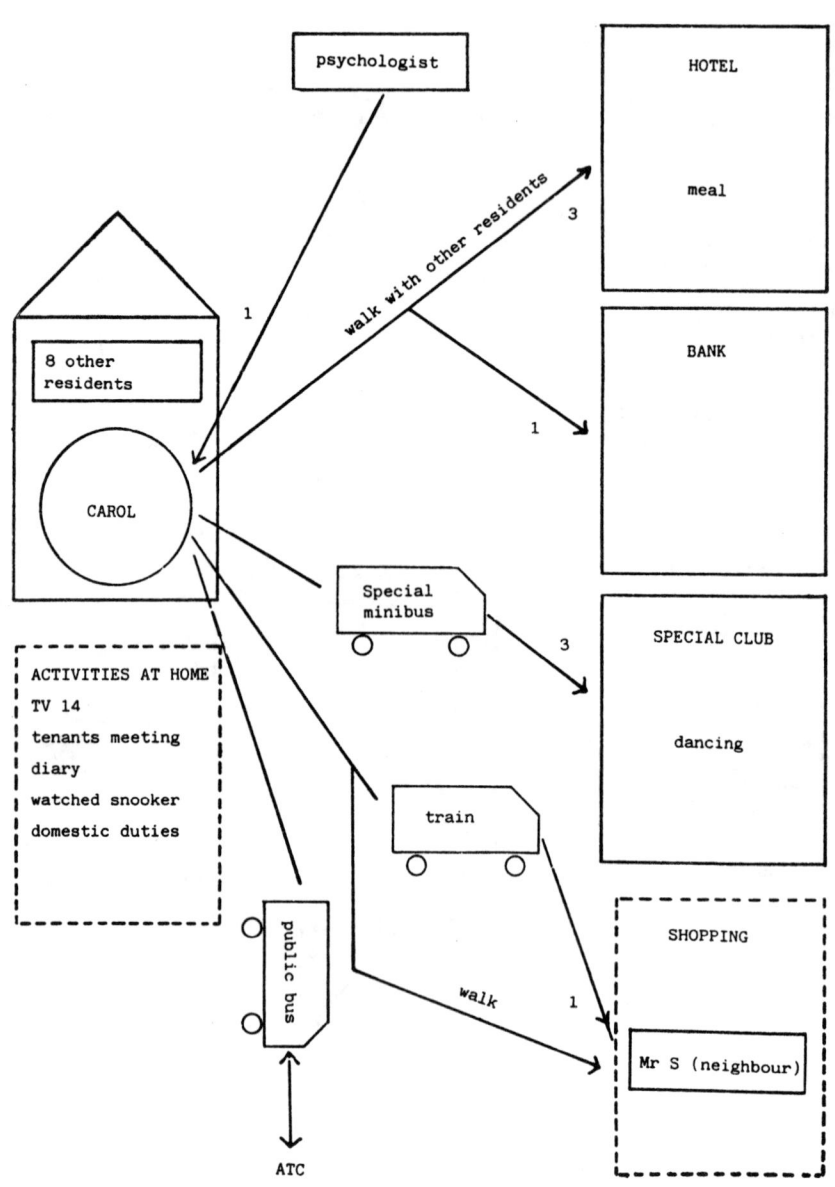

Fig. 4a - Carol, Second Monitored Fortnight (Home-based)

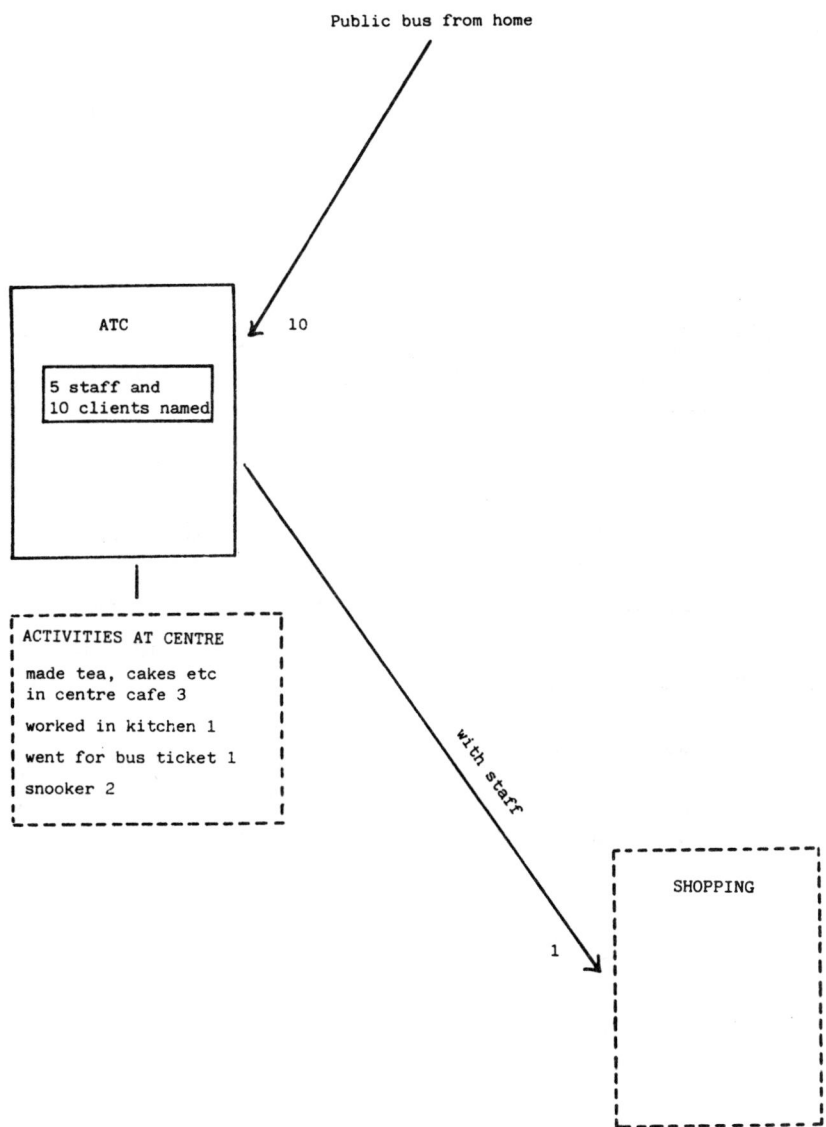

Public bus from home

ATC   10

5 staff and
10 clients named

ACTIVITIES AT CENTRE

made tea, cakes etc
in centre cafe 3

worked in kitchen 1

went for bus ticket 1

snooker 2

with staff

SHOPPING

1

Fig. 4b - Carol, Second Monitored Fortnight (Centre-based)

goes out with staff and friends shopping. She also visits the pub with her key worker.

Carol, like Walter, first attended an adult training centre but she did not get a place at the special project Walter attended. Instead she obtained a place in a further education college attending a one year course. We can see her during the first monitored fortnight travelling a considerable distance by taxi to attend college. She quickly makes friends at college, and these include a Chinese girl whom she meets at lunch time. She certainly enjoyed the college status of being a student. When I spoke to her at this stage she was quite sure she would never want to return to the adult training centre. However, as events turned out this is what happened.

Meantime we can also note that Carol has a boyfriend and this is serious enough for her to meet his mother. The boyfriend and indeed most of Carol's other friends, apart from the Chinese lady, are also from the community of those who have left long-stay mental hospitals. Despite efforts at normalising contacts within the community this tends to happen. Perhaps we should not be surprised. The community, for better or worse, of ex-hospital patients must have strong ties based on past shared experience.

When I next visited Carol she had moved to a voluntary hostel and housing complex. It was new, purpose-built and luxurious. There was a certain amount of controversy about the move. Was it necessary for her to go from a sheltered village to a hostel in order to reach the independent status of having a flat? A flat at the time of the move was not available. When finally she moved to the voluntary hostel she had decided she did not want a flat in any case. She preferred the company and the staff support available there. We can see that for the second monitored fortnight (eighteen months or so after the first) she is visited by a psychologist and, indeed, it is the view of her key worker that such problems as she has which are in terms of her changing moods require psychological or psychiatric help rather than training at a day centre or at a college. Sometimes she feels well and enthusiastic and other days she retreats into herself and complains of feeling ill. With a move from the village to a town some fifteen or twenty miles away the relationship with her boyfriend has ceased. Compared with the intensive village community life, she has relatively few friends outside the house where she stays. She does, however, undertake some journeys by herself to go shopping. She attends another club for handicapped people. She visits the adult training centre each day and travels by public bus. She is encouraged to do this in spite of the fact that this particular centre has organised transport available. Now that she has returned to the adult training centre, Carol says she liked going to college but she also likes the training centre. She regards it as her work and complains that she is not paid sufficiently. She used to do contract work. Now she works in a café associated with the centre and in the kitchen.

It seemed that in Carol's case attendance at the college of further education lifted her up for a while and gave her a status. But the course came to an end and she had not made sufficient progress for anything further to open up as a result of attending. So in terms of day care she returns to the centre she left, which in this case is a centre emphasising the notion of throughput. But throughput to what? Could she get a job? She had one once. Incidentally, she was financially better off when she attended college than she was receiving token wages at the adult training centre.

So Carol has not come on as far as Walter during the same time period since leaving hospital.

However, there is a footnote to this story. After our research finished we learnt that Carol had moved from the adult training centre to attend the same special day project that Walter had previously attended. The period of training within the centre is now complete and she is helping out at a play group three mornings per week and attending the local further education college one day a week.

Points for Discussion

How would you answer the two questions we posed at the beginning of this account, namely:

1. What exactly does community support mean?

2. Is a step-by-step approach to 'independent living' justified?

3. In what ways did the step-by-step approach within the sheltered village prepare Walter for living independently in a house?

4. What is your view about the kind of special project Walter attended as an alternative to an adult training centre? Are there advantages in the project sharing a building with other clubs etc.? Do you think this kind of project could be replicated?*

5. Why do you suppose Carol might not have wanted to have her own flat?

6. Both Walter and Carol have many friends but these tend to be other people who have left hospital. Are such friendships to be accepted, encouraged or discouraged?

7. Do you think Carol has received the kinds of services most appropriate to her needs?

8. How could the uplift Carol received at college be followed through? (It will be noticed that when she returned to the adult training centre her activities were also changed. Previously she had undertaken contract work. But now she worked in a café).

9. What other services might you suggest for Carol?

10. Would you agree that an essential difference between Walter and Carol, at least at the beginning, is that Carol was someone who was basically expecting to be looked after whereas Walter wanted to look after himself? If you had been Carol's key worker, what kinds of suggestions for the future would you have wanted to discuss with her

(i) when she was living in the village and

(ii) now?

11. Do you think that the kind of things that happened to Walter and Carol fifteen years ago could not happen today?

12. What *would* happen today to:

   (i) a young person leaving a children's home, whose parents were unknown and who had not, or could not be, adopted and who had a mild mental handicap?

   (ii) A young person who had an illegitimate child which, it was suggested, she was incapable of looking after and if she also needed some looking after herself?

13. Why do you think that people commonly only find out the details of their past after they have left hospital (or other long-stay institutions)?

14. What could, or should, be done to give people more information about their background while they are in hospital?

15. Certainly Walter, and perhaps Carol, would be regarded as only having mild mental handicaps. Would similar opportunities have been afforded to adults leaving hospital with more severe mental handicaps?

Chapter two

Who cares when carers get older?

What is the role of a day centre for adults with mental handicaps when carers at home are getting older? In this set of two examples, Anne and Joe, we consider this question together with the more general issue of whether people with mental handicaps should move (and, if so, where to?) when the people they depended on for support at home are themselves no longer able to cope without increased support. In the first case, Anne, the carers are the client's father and his housekeeper. In the second example, Joe, the carers are his two sisters.

Anne

Anne is nearly forty. She is more handicapped, in the sense of being disadvantaged in daily living, than the clients we have so far discussed. Yet her specific abilities vary, and any 'IQ' assessment could be misleading. It would cover up the wide differences in Anne's abilities in different kinds of situations. For example, while Anne cannot handle money in the sense of being able to go into a shop, select the correct money for articles when she does not know the price beforehand, and check the change afterwards, she can add up sums in an exercise book. She can read and write to a limited extent, and sufficient for normal daily living. She completed parts of her own diaries for the research. Yet she has problems with toileting (on account of a physical complaint) and she could not prepare, by herself, a simple meal.

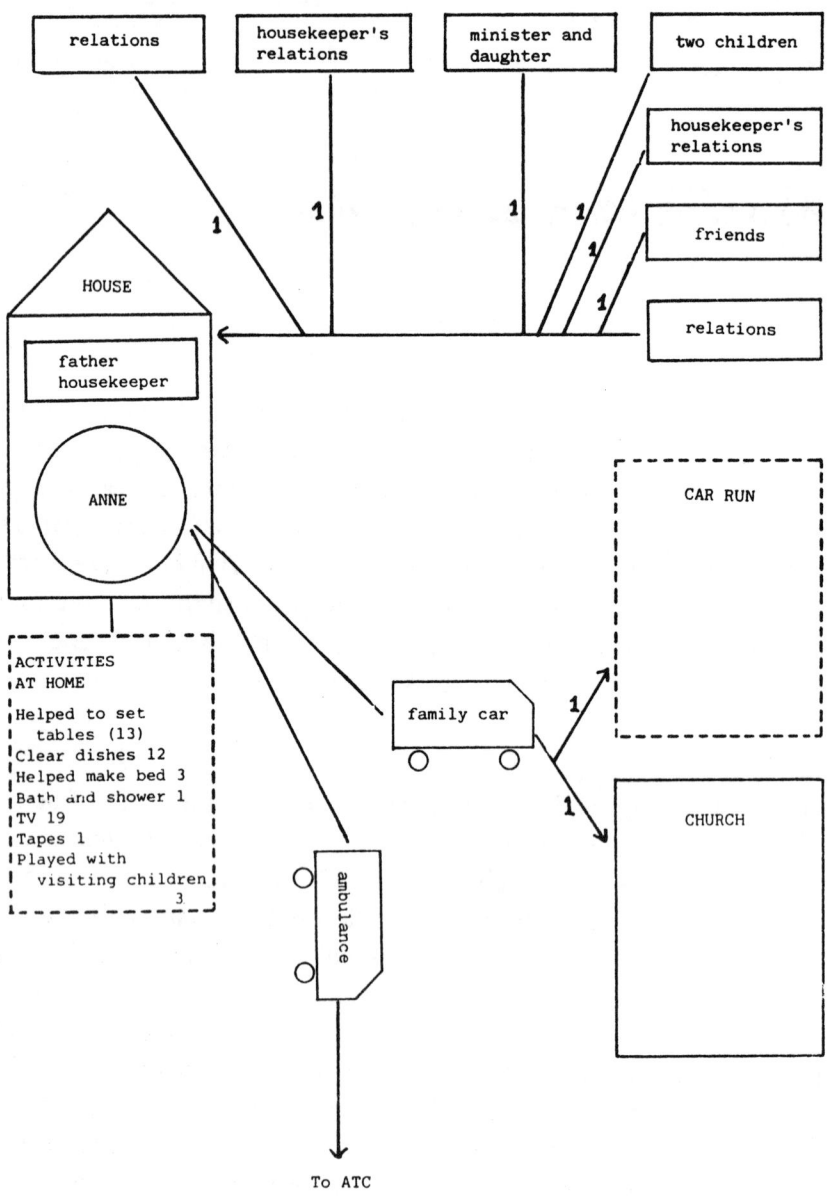

Fig. 5a - Anne, First Monitored Fortnight (Home-based)

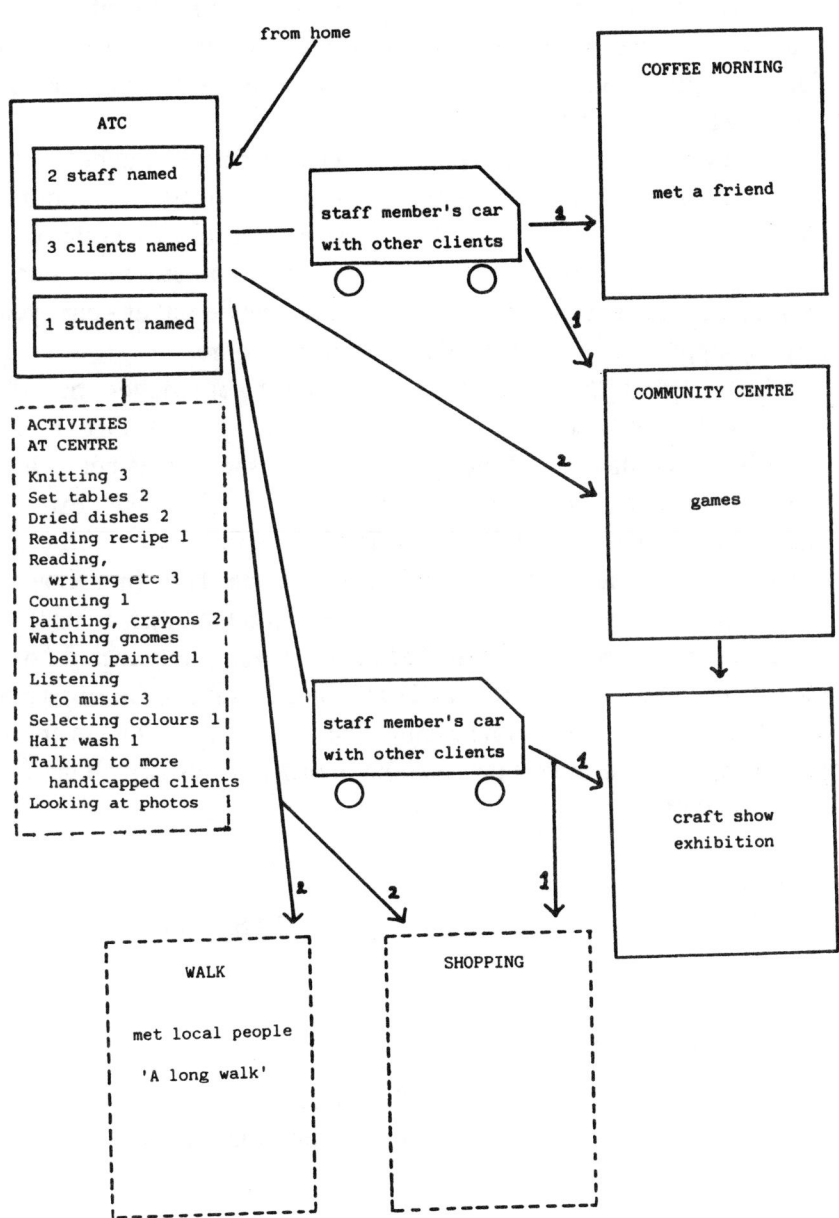

Fig. 5b - Anne, First Monitored Fortnight (Centre-based)

Anne has made great progress recently in learning specific tasks. During the course of the research, for example, she learnt a lot of new things, ranging from floating on her back in the swimming pool to brushing her own teeth.

Anne was for many years a patient in a day hospital for people with mental handicaps. For a short while, some years ago, after her mother died, she became an in-patient. But Anne was so distressed at this that her father moved house, on professional advice, to a place where a small local adult training centre was available. Meanwhile father employed a housekeeper who helps to look after Anne at home.

The father's initial expectations of the centre were modest, namely that it would 'keep her happy'. During the research period, not only did Anne learn the things we have mentioned, but she *was*, as her father put it, 'happier than she had ever been in her life before'. Her experience at the centre is shown in *figure five* for the first monitored fortnight. It was similar in the second fortnight, a year later (not shown) except that Anne now went out from home (accompanied), for example to church or to the shops. Yet, as the following examples selected from the list of activities at the centre and staff objectives show, the emphasis of staff at the centre is less on learning than on enabling Anne to enjoy life to the full. Learning is perhaps the product of this aim being fulfilled, rather than the starting point.

ACTIVITIES	OBJECTIVES and COMMENTS
Listening to music.	Enjoyment.
Watching school sports.	She likes to watch people doing things she cannot do herself.

Watching more able clients.	She enjoys it. She enjoys company. Opportunity to be in a smaller group which she likes.
Washing clothes.	To help her to learn to do it for herself.
Gardening.	To follow through the fact that she volunteered.
Hygiene.	To get her to do as much as she can for herself.
Outings.	Enjoyment. Takes her out into the community.
Games at community centre.	To get her moving. She likes it.
Reading.	To help her from falling back at reading. She likes to read.

Anne's father is getting older and less fit. The housekeeper is also elderly. What will happen to Anne in the longer-term? Is the centre preparing Anne for the future? She is being given some domestic training and training in hygiene to help her to be more independent. Is this sufficient? The father (and probably the centre staff) would never see Anne as being able to manage without constant care. Given this view, what does training for 'independence' mean?

During the research, a home-help was introduced to help look after the father. This might help to postpone the time when decisions about Anne's future will have to be taken. But, in the long-term, Anne is likely to outlive her father and the kinds of questions we have raised will have to be faced. Should they be faced sooner rather than later?

Before discussing the alternatives, we will introduce the second example, Joe.

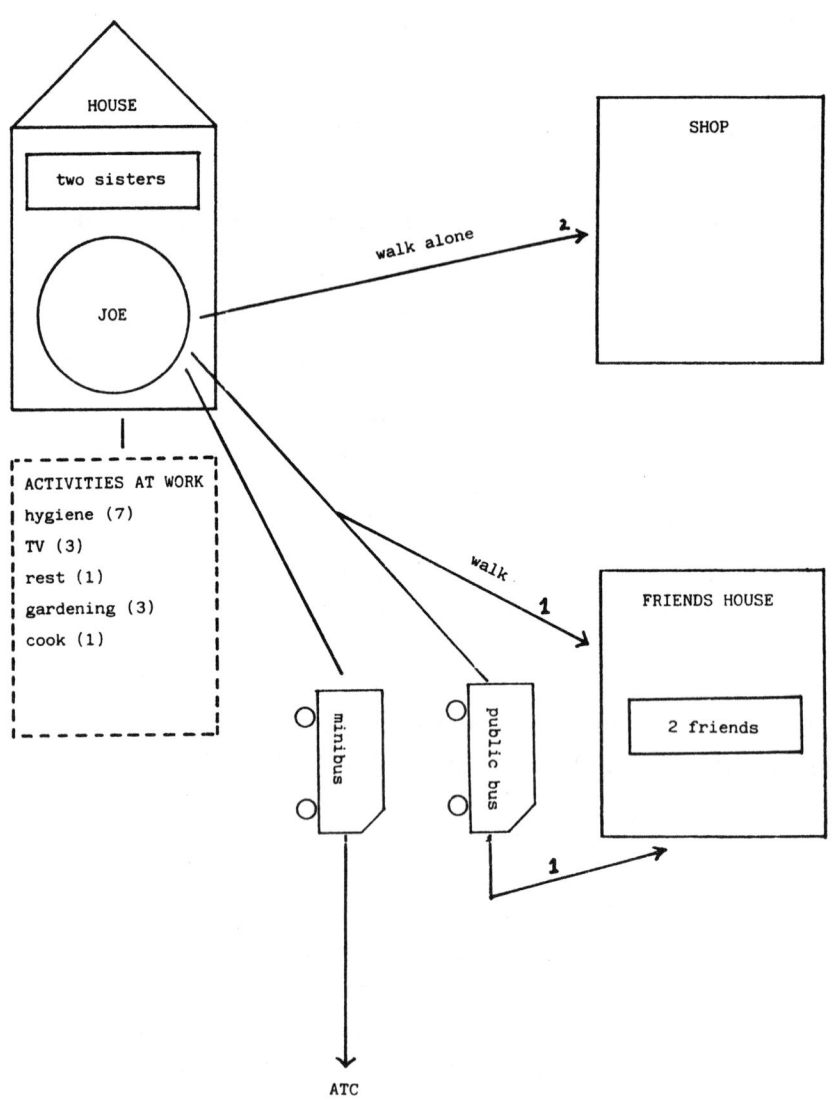

Fig. 6a - Joe, First Monitored Fortnight (Home-based)

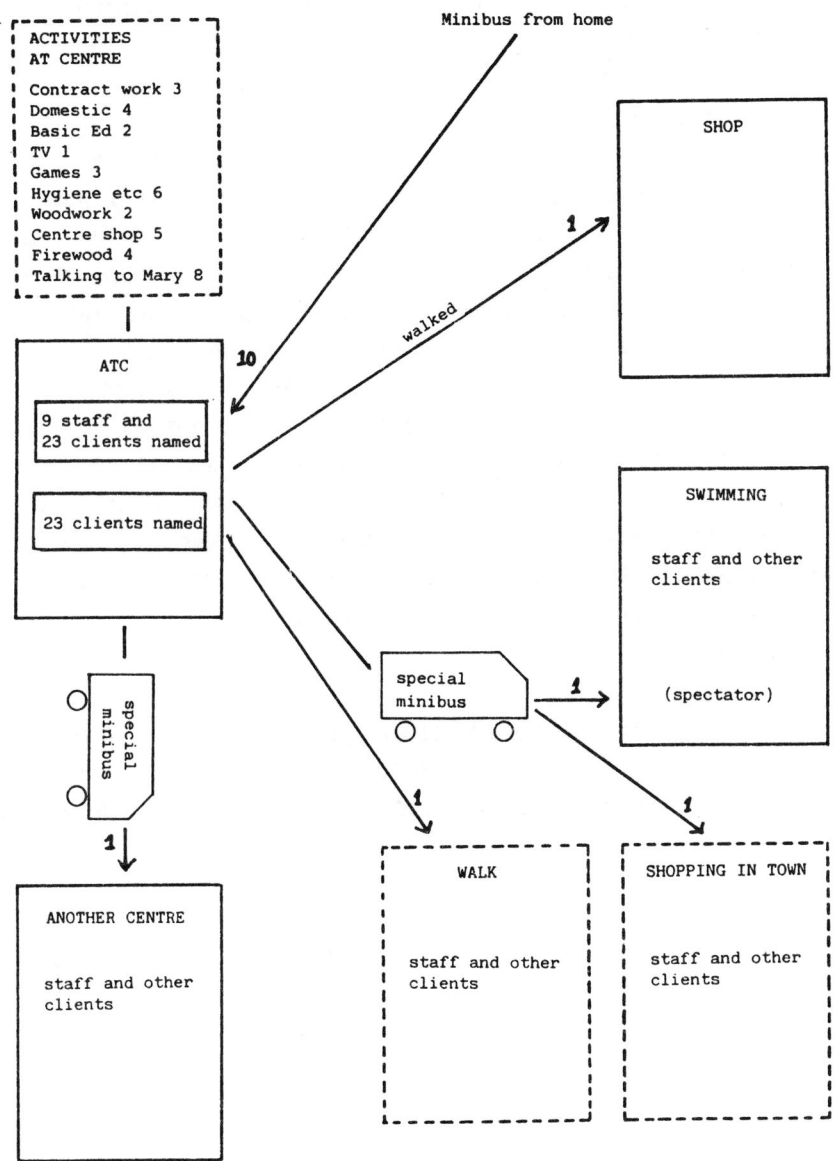

ACTIVITIES
AT CENTRE

Contract work 3
Domestic 4
Basic Ed 2
TV 1
Games 3
Hygiene etc 6
Woodwork 2
Centre shop 5
Firewood 4
Talking to Mary 8

Minibus from home

SHOP

ATC

10

walked   1

9 staff and
23 clients named

23 clients named

SWIMMING

staff and other
clients

(spectator)   1

special
minibus   1

special
minibus

ANOTHER CENTRE

staff and other
clients

1

WALK

staff and other
clients

1

SHOPPING IN TOWN

staff and other
clients

1

Fig. 6b - Joe, First Monitored Fortnight (Centre-based)

Joe

Joe is in his early sixties and his two sisters are considerably older. Both of the sisters suffer from chronic illness. Joe himself was said to be epileptic, but no fits were reported during the research.

Joe left school at fourteen and worked for a few months at a fish processing factory. He then had other part-time jobs. After his father died, he lived with his brother and mother. When the brother married and the mother died he came to live with his two sisters. This illustrates a fairly common pattern. Adults with handicaps may move from one relation to another within an extended family. We have found examples of this happening in our research in rural areas in particular.

What is the role of the centre in Joe's situation? Joe says he attends because he likes it. His sisters' general view is that the centre keeps him busy, and that it is of benefit to them insofar as they are then less worried about him. It will be noticed from the diagram for the first monitored fortnight (*figure six*) that Joe's activities range from contract work and woodwork to basic education and hygiene. Hygiene is particularly important in so far as the sisters are concerned because, they say, Joe gets his bath at the centre and they are no longer able to give it to him at home.

Joe did not keep full enough diaries for us to draw a diagram for the second monitored fortnight but we do have information from the centre list of activities and the objectives and comments from staff. These are as follows:

ACTIVITIES	OBJECTIVES and COMMENTS
Art.	Enjoyment.
Craft.	To improve skills.

Woodwork.	He enjoys it. To improve and extend skills. Maybe to help at home.
Kitchen duties.	To help him share chores with other clients.
Training kitchen.	To improve skills. To learn about appropriate equipment. (A problem is the lack of appropriate equipment). To help at home.
Visit to Garden Centre.	Choosing and collecting equipment. To extend existing skills. (Problem of lack of time for such visits).
Shopping.	He enjoys it. Integration into the community.
Disco.	To be beside Mary (friend).
Sex education.	To make him aware of different aspects of sexuality.
Basic education.	To improve basic skills. This is hardly necessary at his age.
Chopping wood.	He enjoys it. Occupies him.
Gardening	He enjoys it. Maybe it will help.

It will be noticed that Joe's programme has quite substantially changed since the first monitored fortnight, following a review at the centre. The sisters, however, were not consulted about these changes and when we interviewed them during the second monitored fortnight and asked for their opinion on each of the activities, they thought the gardening was excellent but, on the other hand, the exclusion of hygiene, and especially the bath or shower was 'deplorable'. His weekly baths had stopped, they said and his toe-nails needed cutting. They were too elderly to do these things for him.

The centre was giving more attention to Joe's social needs. Shopping was described as a means of integration into the community.

Joe has a particular friend of the opposite sex at the centre. She is called Mary. The staff recognise the importance of this relationship and it will be seen from the list of activities and objectives for the second monitored fortnight that the comment beside 'Disco' was that Joe could 'be beside Mary'. He is also receiving sex education 'to make him aware of different aspects of sexuality'. However, there is no indication that Joe and Mary intend to live together.

What, then, is the future for Joe? When I raised this question with Joe's sisters, the reply was one of astonishment that such a question should be asked. They assumed that he would 'go on to help somebody else'.

Joe has spent twenty nine years attending an adult training centre. Is there an assumption that, perhaps at sixty five, he will leave? If so, why and what will be the alternative? What will the sisters think of this? If not, what is the continuing role of the centre in Joe's old age? In any case, is the programme of centre activities and staff objectives relevant to Joe's present and future needs?

Points for Discussion

1. Would any of the following possibilities be appropriate in considering either Anne or Joe's long-term future? (This list is based on other examples from research).

    (a) Move to other members of the extended family.

    (b) Stay on in present house with support, taking on tenancy or ownership. (What support would be needed?)

DAILY STAFF DIARY REGARDING Joe COMPLETED BY Kerry DAY Wed..... DATE 17/4

	DURING THE MORNING	LUNCH	DURING THE AFTERNOON
LIST ACTIVITIES:	Was quiet as usual during Tutorial. Hygiene for 1st period. Mr Clark swapping Shirts in garage		Had a shower and hair trim with Mr Williamson
STAFF EXPECTATIONS REGARDING EACH ACTIVITY	Good worker and helper		No problem. Needs a chiropodist
STAFF COMMENTS ON FULFILMENT OR NON-FULFILMENT OF EXPECTATIONS	Placid and consistent		Very helpful regarding other trainees. Fetches towels, soap and powder without having to be asked
OTHER COMMENTS CONCERNING CLIENT, e.g. BEHAVIOUR, ATTITUDE, MOOD	Good		No trouble at all

Figure 7

(c) Hospitalisation. Some parents or other carers like to see this as a 'fall-back' possibility. (Is this likely to apply to Anne or Joe?)

(d) Hostel or other residential setting.

(e) Shared sheltered housing. This is an idea being considered by the Cornerstone Society for the Mentally Handicapped in Aberdeen. The person with a handicap shares sheltered housing with an ageing carer. The balance of who depends on whom changes and support is given to both carer and client. When the original carer dies, the client will continue to be supported.

2. Joe was at home, intermittently working, until he was in his late twenties. At that time the adult training centre was newly opened and was looking for clients. Do you think any other alternatives could have been considered at the time? What, if any, alternatives would be available today?

3. What would be the continued role now, if any, of day services for Anne and for Joe?

4. What other services are needed in relation to any of the above possibilities?

5. Would you want to know an IQ figure in deciding what to do in the best interests of Anne or Joe? If not, what other forms of assessment would be most useful?

6. Do you think the promotion of the client's happiness is a good starting point in considering centre staff objectives in these two cases?

7. In Joe's case how do you weigh up the advantages or possible disadvantages of what is perhaps a more focused programme in terms of preparation for independent living, with the carers' complaint about the lack of support to them when they stopped giving Joe a bath?

(Staff comments on this activity while it was taking place are shown in *figure seven*).

8. One centre known to us (not any of the ones in this discussion) has started 'carers' discussion groups'. What do you think of the idea? Is this best organised through the centre, or by an independent parents' group?

Postscript

After the research finished we learnt that Anne had begun a process of introduction to a hostel, so that she will be prepared for a possible future move from home.

Chapter three

Does elderly mean handicapped?

In the previous set of examples, we looked at elderly carers. We now look at the situations of clients with mental handicaps whose original carers have died and who are themselves becoming older. Do adult training centres cater for people who are 'elderly'? Most centres think not and therefore the staff think in terms of clients 'retiring' at some stage. But, we may ask, retiring from what, and for what? What is their future?

In this set of three examples we apply these general questions more specifically to situations of people who, in fact, managed to live a long time in the community without day care. The question of day care arose only when their parents died.

William

William is in his early sixties. A few years before we first met him he was living with his brother, who was ill. William helped look after him. William was less and less able to cope and, apparently, he was locally regarded as an oddity, spending a lot of his time wandering about local streets and parks. Eventually he was admitted, as an emergency, to a home for the elderly, which catered for a total of fifty-five residents. Only after this was he introduced, for the first time in his life, to an adult training centre.

The home and the centre are quite close together and William walks to the centre every day - although he says on wet days he can catch the bus.

Figure eight gives us a picture of a fortnight in the life of William in the home for the elderly and attending the adult training centre.

William is not in any way physically disabled. He is able to go out for a walk by himself to watch football. It is, therefore, in his case, superfluous for an orchestra and a church minister to visit him at 'home' although it might be helpful for some of the other residents who could be physically incapacitated. The question may also be asked for someone of his age, who has not previously attended special facilities for those with mental handicaps, what mental handicap means? For the first sixty years of his life he was probably not generally thought of as such. Why, then, should he suddenly be thought of as having a mental handicap when he gets older?

William can read and write a little. Staff at the centre claim he does not understand the use of money. William himself says he can use the bus to get to the centre on wet days. Otherwise, as he wrote down for us, he walks to the centre every day. He chats to the lollipop lady *en route*.

Apart from the lollipop lady, it will be seen that William has no friends outside the institutional life of home and centre. If it is true, as is suspected, that he had no friends other than his brother before he was admitted to the home, certainly he has not found any since. He has, however, made friends with other residents and other people with handicaps at the centre.

What is the centre aiming to do, and in fact doing, for William? The network diagram shows that first of all it is taking him out with other people with handicaps in special transport or the instructor's car. He visits an exhibition, a transport museum, a convent and also a hospital for people with mental handicaps where he meets 'other clients' friends'. Once he goes to the shops.

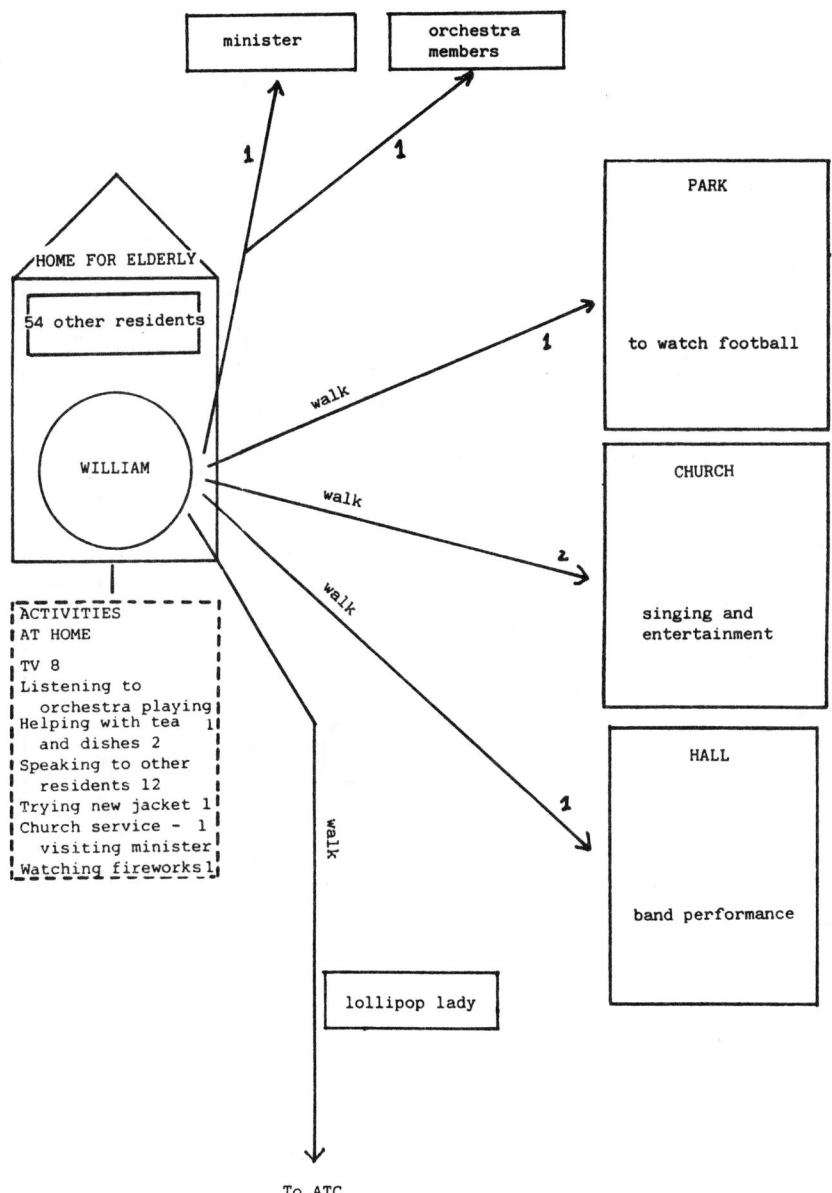

Fig. 8a - William, First Monitored Fortnight (Home-based)

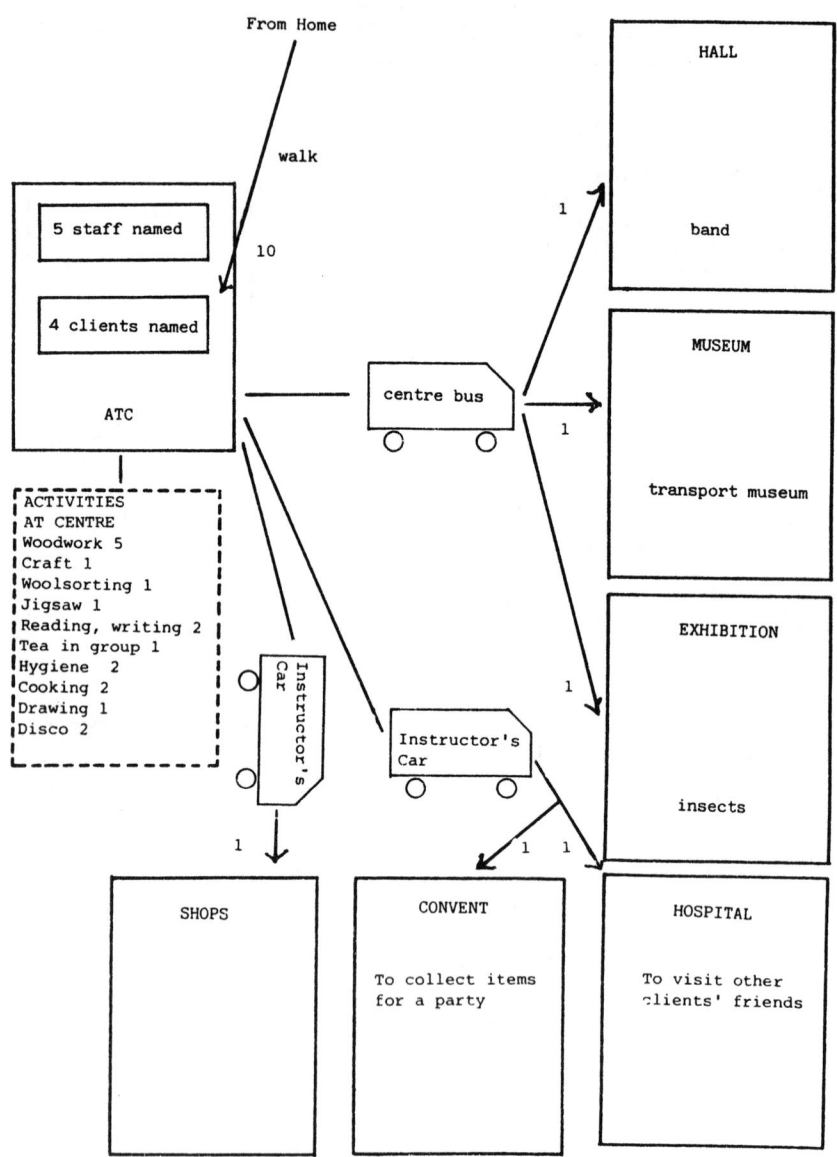

Fig. 8b - William, First Monitored Fortnight (Centre-based)

We looked in detail at what William was doing at the day centre and what the day centre staff were trying to do for him. We give below three separate accounts of a typical day during the first monitored fortnight. Firstly, we have William's account, as recorded by a member of the staff at the Home. Secondly, we have William's account as recorded by a member of staff at the centre for the same day and, finally, we have an account by members of staff speaking for themselves about their objectives for each activity undertaken during that day.

25th October

1. William's account (recorded at the old people's Home).

Dressed, waited to see if rain went off. Spoke to my friends Harry and Tom. (After attending centre): hurried home in case I got wet. Nodded to someone who knows me. Ate supper, watched TV and watched the orchestra in the House. Spoke to Jim (resident) and asked how he was keeping.

2. William's account (recorded by staff at centre).

William said it was not far to walk. He would have taken a bus if it had been wet. He said he did not know the cost. He said he was on his own when walking. He walked past people. 'When I arrived, I took off my coat and had a seat. I had a cup of tea and then went to the education room. I did reading and writing.' He said he was a good writer. (After details of what happened at lunch time): 'I was with Michael, big tall bloke, with red hair like a cowboy ...'. He had a bath and shave and felt refreshed. Then he said he felt sleepy and hungry. He said that in the education room 'It is just like sitting in school. If I get too much money I get mixed up'. William reckons he did not go out on a trip today with the others because it was too wet. (At the end of being interviewed by the staff to complete the diary he asked if he had answered the questions 'quite good'. He said: 'You can't do any more than your best.')

3. Staff account of activities and objectives for William at the centre.

ACTIVITIES	**OBJECTIVES and COMMENTS**
Reading.	William arrived late. He explained the story to me. Then he had a cup of tea in the group.
Hygiene - brushing his teeth, having a bath, washing his hair.	I hoped that William would learn to keep himself clean and tidy. The Hygiene worked well. He does not thoroughly brush his teeth.
Crafts. He did a jig-saw and was working with wool.	I hoped that with the wool he would be able to distinguish colours. The wool was a bit of a disaster. He could not distinguish most shades. He was in a very good and happy mood. His behaviour is never any problem.

Between the two monitored fortnights we visited William at the Home for the elderly. I was told that he was going to the centre later and later. This was because he liked to get his cup of tea at the Home before he left. I was also told that his sister had died. It was also reported that William helps another resident in the Home to go through to breakfast and that he is friendly with others.

Meanwhile I had interviewed William himself. When we asked him why he went to the adult training centre he said 'because I was put there'. He added that it was to pass the time of day. He said 'time flies if you are working'. I asked him what he had learnt there and he said he had learnt to sandpaper and also to cook food. But he added 'I could cook before. My brother and I used to take turns about'. His favourite activity, he told me, at the centre was cooking. He said 'I get to take cakes home'. He said he would like to go to the centre more often rather than less often and at weekends too but for parties, not work. He would like more parties and dances at the centre.

The following is a summary of the activities undertaken, and comments from staff, during the second monitored fortnight:

ACTIVITIES	OBJECTIVES and COMMENTS
Domestic.	Enjoyment. He tends to take over, seeming to know it all, e.g. peeling potatoes and using the washing machine.
Hygiene: Had a bath and shave.	Eventually hope he'll he able to do it himself without prompting. He tends to come in unshaven. He enjoys being told to shave. A problem is lack of space for this activity and the group is too large for the room.
Outings.	For enjoyment and seeing other people.
Disco.	Mixing. He tends to be a loner.
Reading and writing.	No real aim because of his age and ability. He enjoys education and he is strong in this area. He is of an age where he is not

going to change. He has everything catered for him at home.

Workshop: constructing little kits - sanding and varnishing.	To give him something to do and keep him interested. He can do these things. But he builds them all wrong and you try to tell him how to do it but usually you have to do it for him. It is cramped as a workshop, used for putting things out. It gets cluttered up.
Horse riding lesson.	Company - rather than being on his own. He wouldn't go on a horse. I don't know if there's many people that would take the time to talk to him.
Helping to organise layout for dance.	Just something for him to do.
Various errands in connection with the evening dance (in place of another activity).	Something for him to do.
Visit to swimming baths.	Enjoys spectating - asks to go to swimming. Enjoys cup of tea.
Educational outing in minibus. (Visited park and then anotheradult training centre)	Something to do. He tends to get isolated a lot. He arrives very late so that it's hard to get him started in the group. He wants the toilet as soon as he goes anywhere. His age means there's not a lot we can do with him educationally.

Outing to swimming baths - because of gala being held the next day	Enjoyment as spectator. To get him out. This is the only group he will willingly take part in.
	Final staff comment: William won't go into a group at all. I spoke to the manager about this and was told as long as he is just getting a break, not to push him.

After the second monitored fortnight I discussed with William's key worker at the Home what were the important places and people were in his life. The important places were a church hall, local shows and watching football in the park. Important people were the lollipop lady and staff at the Home. The lollipop lady was important to him as a friend, rather than offering any kind of help. He chats to her on 'dry days'.

Points for Discussion

1. William is in an old people's home with fifty-four other residents. Is this the most appropriate setting? What alternatives could there be?

2. Is there any evidence of the effects of institutionalisation on William?

3. Should William be at an adult training centre? What would be the alternatives? Should William have gone to a centre earlier in his life?

4. Granted that William *is* attending an adult training centre, what would you suggest as an individualised plan which is more constructive than simply finding him 'something to do'?

5. Comment on the choice and relevance of each of the activities and objectives listed.

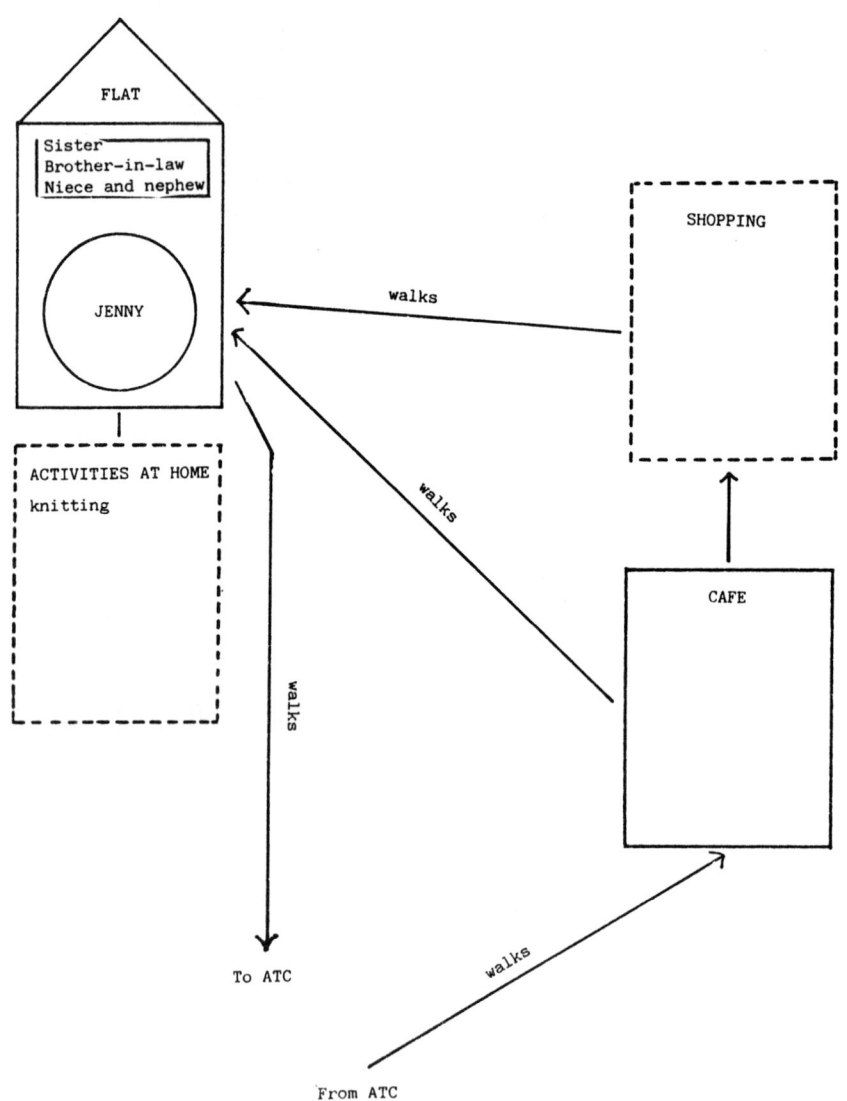

Fig. 9a - Jenny, First Monitored Fortnight (Home-based)

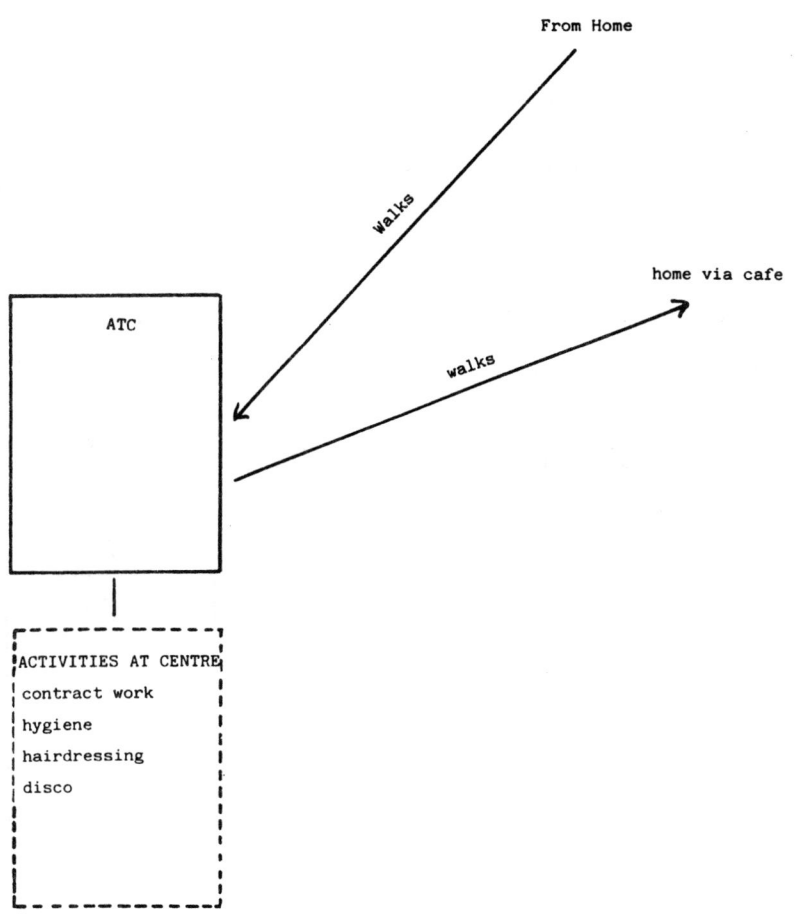

Fig. 9b - Jenny, First Monitored Fortnight (Centre-based)

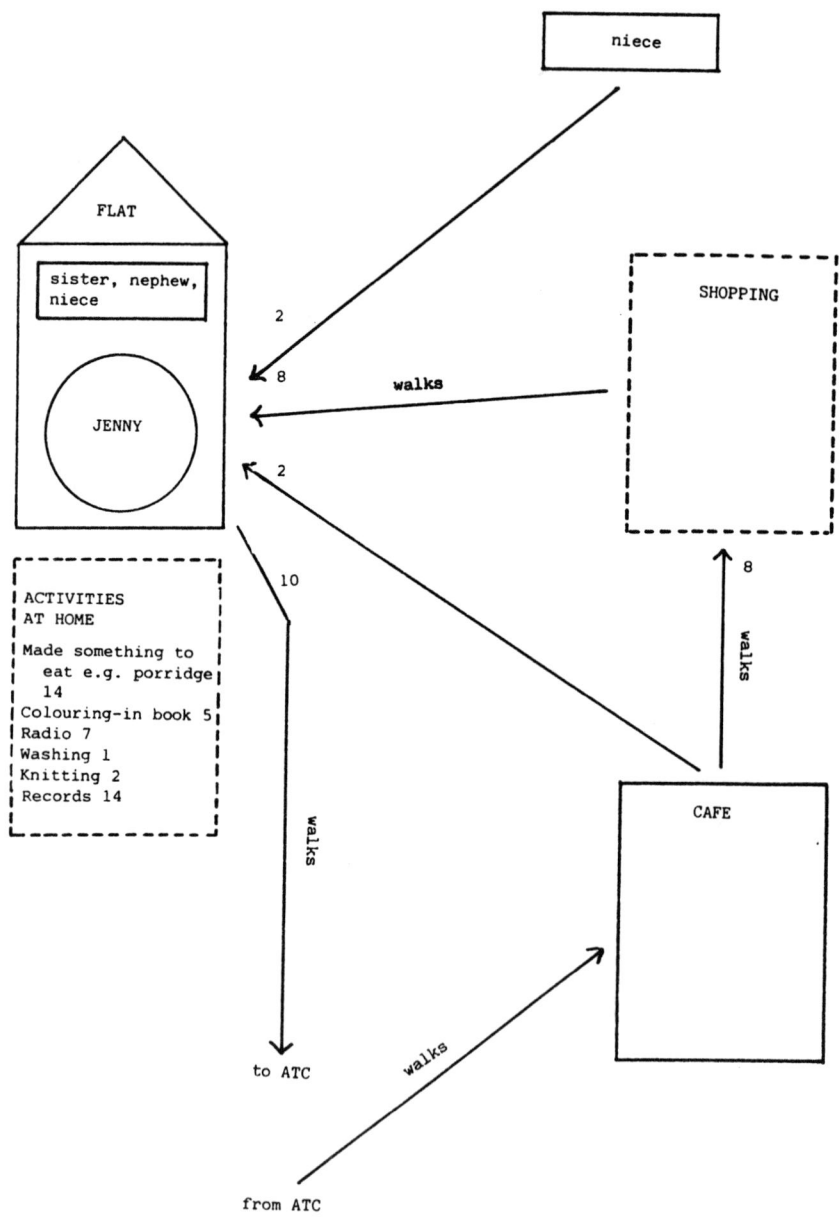

Fig. 10a - Jenny, Second Monitored Fortnight (Home-based)

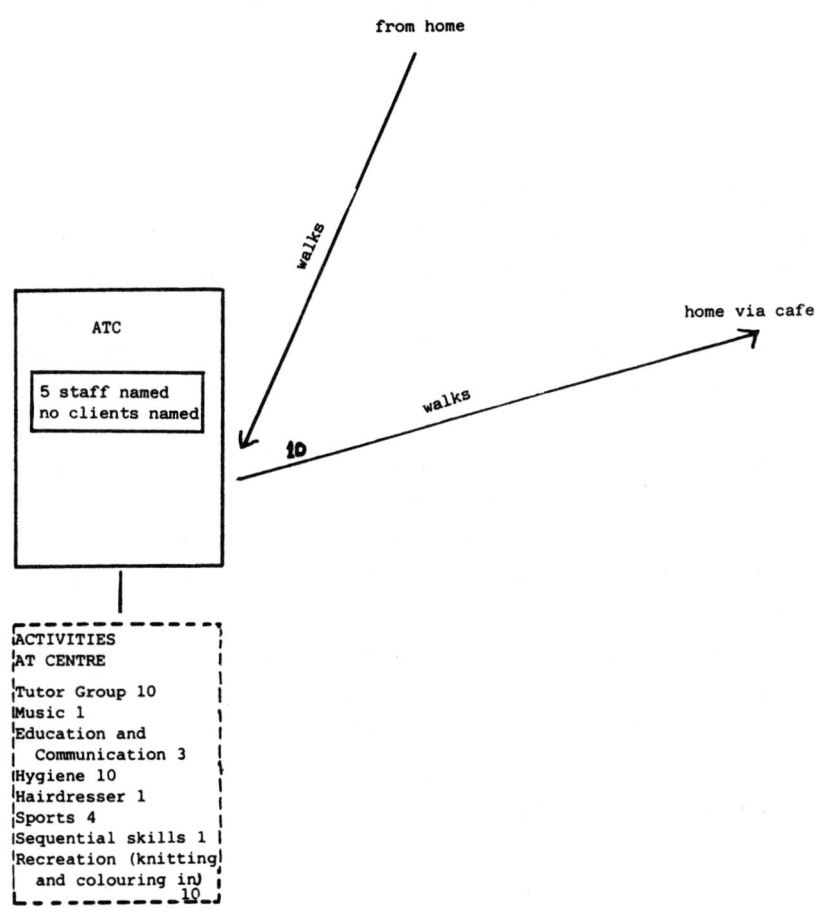

from home

walks

ATC

5 staff named
no clients named

home via cafe

walks

10

ACTIVITIES
AT CENTRE

Tutor Group 10
Music 1
Education and
 Communication 3
Hygiene 10
Hairdresser 1
Sports 4
Sequential skills 1
Recreation (knitting
 and colouring in)
 10

Fig. 10b - Jenny, Second Monitored Fortnight (Centre-based)

6. Do you accept that for someone of William's age, it is too late to learn? William does seem to be making friends. How do you evaluate the possibilities for using these friendships as a basis for enabling William to lead a more independent life?

Jenny

Jenny is about ten years younger than William. When we first knew her she lived as a lodger with her sister, brother-in-law and their children. The sister explained that Jenny liked to be independent, keeping herself to herself. She said they used to be more involved in trying to keep Jenny clean, but they had not had to do this since Jenny had been taught hygiene at the adult training centre. Before coming to the centre, relatively late in her life, Jenny (like William) had wandered in the streets.

Jenny's abilities are somewhat similar to William's. She can prepare a simple meal, use public transport and undertake simple domestic chores. She is less able than William in expressing herself. According to her sister, Jenny tends to panic when, for example, she gets a letter from the DHSS.

We can see from the network diagrams for the first and second monitored fortnights (See *figures nine* and *ten*) that Jenny leads a restricted social life, doing only necessary shopping on the way back home from the centre. She has no friends outside the centre.

Between the first and second monitored fortnights, Jenny's brother-in-law died. For a few weeks after this she seemed to slide beck into a more slovenly personal appearance. But by the time of the second monitoring she had recovered and was taking part in a greater variety of centre activities. It may be, also, that the centre staff were becoming more aware of her needs. It seems they now had a concerted plan to prepare Jenny to be more independent as she became older. Below is a summary of the activities and staff objectives and comments for the second monitored fortnight.

ACTIVITIES	OBJECTIVES and COMMENTS
Hygiene. Washing her clothing.	To teach her to do for herself. General learning. To take her out to the launderette.
Hairdressing.	To teach her to do it on her own in a hand-basin. (She can already do it in a shower at the centre, but she does not have a shower at home).
Sewing. Care and repair of clothes.	To be able to sew a button and sewfor herself.
Basic education. Reading and writing. Social sight vocabulary (e.g. signs).	
Shopping.	To improve and reinforce shopping skills. To learn correct use of money.
Games.	To motivate her. Otherwise she tends to sit and draw.
Cookery.	To improve cooking skills. To improve her knowledge of cookery, including being able to compare prices of items.
Musical movement with exercises.	To increase her co-ordination.

| | from the crowd. |
| Music and singing. | Stimulant. Relaxing. She is inclined to curl into herself. Withdrawn. |

While much is done to improve her 'survival' skills at the centre, little attention appears to be paid to her lack of social life outside the centre. Yet the question must arise, does Jenny want her social life enriched? Once I asked her if she had any particular friends and she replied: 'No, I keep myself to myself.' Yet she is not without interest in other people and places. She is fond of knitting. Although this did not feature as an activity in the list of centre activities, she could often be found during the lunch break knitting squares for Ethiopian refugees. She also told me she had enjoyed a recent centre holiday because they were 'out all the time'.

Points for Discussion

1. Is it desirable to involve Jenny in activities with other people in the community, and not just within the centre ? If so, how would you set about doing this?

2. Many centres recognise a 'retirement' age for their clients (perhaps sixty or sixty-five). Yet, it could be argued, as Jenny becomes older she will need more, not less, support. Would you consider some other form of day care for the elderly? If so, what would be the difference? Would this benefit Jenny?

3. Do you think Jenny's programme of activities at the centre will help to prevent an otherwise likely admission to a Home for the elderly? Do you think it possible for Jenny to continue to live in a flat on her own as she gets older and, perhaps, not live with her sister? If so, what kind of support at home would she need and who would provide it?

4. Do you see any greater reasons for William to be in a Home for the elderly than Jenny say, in ten years' time? If not, what advantages has Jenny had that William did not have?

5. At the moment, Jenny's sister is willing to offer support, but it is claimed that Jenny herself seeks a measure of independence. The sister also has other members of her own family to care for. Would you suggest working with Jenny to help her to accept support from her sister? Alternatively, would you encourage Jenny to leave her sister's house? Or would you just leave things at home as they are?

6. Would William benefit from the kind of centre programme Jenny had (perhaps earlier in his life)?

Jessie

Jessie is nearly sixty. Like William and Jenny, it is only in the later part of her life that she has come to attend a day centre. Unlike William and Jenny, however, she was known to be handicapped from a very young age.

Jessie's sister also has a handicap, as does her sister's daughter (Jessie's niece), with whom she now lives. All three attended the same residential special school. When they left school the two sisters were at first supported by their parents and when their parents died members of the extended family helped. A neighbour of the family was, and still is, also involved in giving support. The niece was regarded by the researcher as the main support person at home - though in different ways they helped each other.

The day centre Jessie attends is an unusual one. It grew out of a club which Jessie and her niece attended. It is different from the traditional idea of an 'adult training centre' in two main respects. Firstly, part-time attendance is normal and in this instance Jessie and her niece attend on different days. Jessie particularly enjoys coming on a day which is set aside for an afternoon club. She also attends on another day when there is more emphasis on social learning. Secondly, the centre sets out

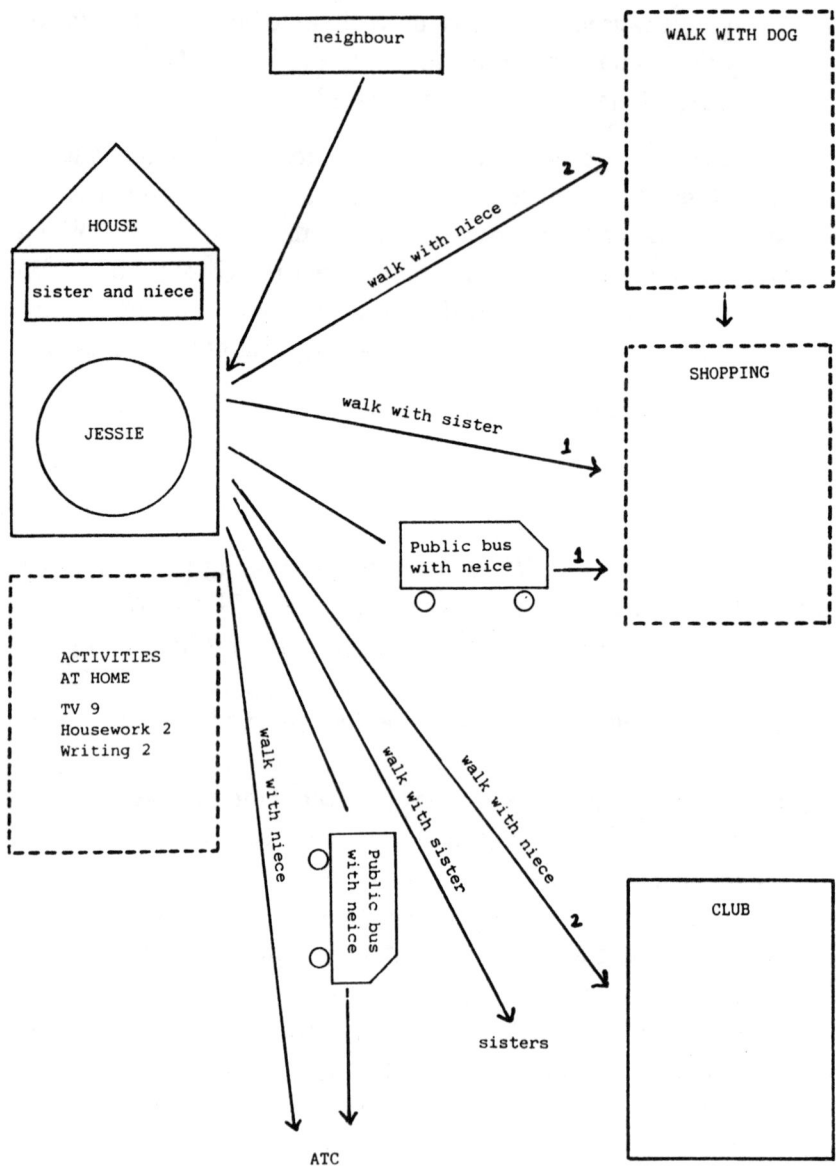

Fig. 11a - Jessie, First Monitored Fortnight (Home-based)

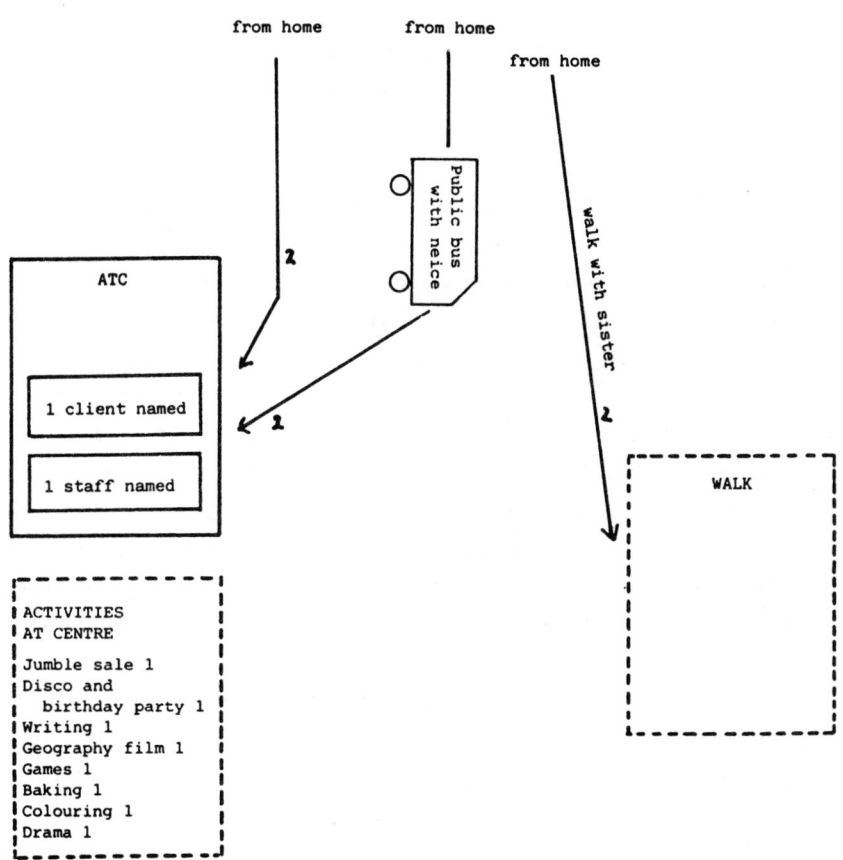

Fig. 11b - Jessie, First Monitored Fortnight (Centre-based)

to be a resource, linking together other resources in the immediate neighbourhood to help people with mental handicaps in direct and practical ways.

Figure eleven shows Jessie's pattern of living at home and her activities at the centre for the first monitored fortnight. The diagram for the second monitored fortnight (not shown) included visits also from the social worker and health visitor as well as the neighbour. The social worker takes care of Jessie and her sister's money. The niece teaches Jessie how to read and write and tell the time. It was the niece who kept the diaries for Jessie.

The researcher felt that quite dramatic improvements were made between the first and second monitored fortnights. This was due partly to the stimulation and activities received at the centre and partly, and more subtly, to the part played by the centre in promoting the network of support at home and in the neighbourhood as a whole. Perhaps the recording undertaken by the staff at the centre does not always do justice to this 'community' aspect of their work because it is not in terms of 'instruction' or other direct activities with clients at the centre. It is in terms of keeping in touch with people, using informal opportunities to put people in touch with each other and maintaining contact with other services.

What does come across in the comments of the staff is the importance of the social function a centre can perform for someone like Jessie. For example, Jessie, during the first monitored fortnight, had to perform at her birthday party. She was, said the staff, 'very happy and enjoyed singing a song in front of the group. She always enjoys a party and if asked will get up and sing with absolutely no embarrassment. We made a video of her singing and she was overjoyed to see it played back to her'. There is, however, an educational side to the centre activities. The purpose of baking was 'being able to measure and mix well'. By the time of the second monitored fortnight the educational tasks were more sophisticated. She baked a few small cakes, and she was said to be 'very good at this'. An education morning was spent 'learning to listen' in relation to writing. The object was to try to get Jessie to write more clearly and learn addresses without needing to copy. It was reported, however, that she was 'still copying only'. Some of the activities, with an educational purpose, were informal and spontaneous. For example, she was 'tidying up her geography folder' in order 'to encourage awareness of the world outside'. The centre manager's comments on Jessie's features of performance was that she 'accomplishes something new every day and is growing in confidence all the time'. The researcher added: 'This too is my impression and I feel the centre works particularly positively for Jessie in this respect. It is perhaps ironic that I am saying this for a woman nearly sixty years old, rather than for the younger clients. After leaving school Jessie was at home from 1940-1981 and I wonder how many other Jessies there are unknown to the authorities, who could perhaps benefit from a similar service, albeit at a younger stage in their lives'. The neighbour who offers practical and social support is not in any way related but she has known the family for many years in an area where neighbourliness still counts.

Points for Discussion

1. This centre appears to be very different from the others we have considered. How far does centre practice in this case differ from the routines of the traditional ATC you would expect? Would Jessie have benefited from the centres attended by William and Jenny (so far as we can tell from the examples given)? Would there have been any differences in the way you would have approached William's situation, or Jenny's situation, had you been the manager or a staff person at Jessie's centre?

2. This is an instance of people with handicaps supporting each other in the context of support they are receiving from outside. The family unit has continued to function after the death of the parents. Do you think this is a good idea? What would be the alternatives? (The

answers to these questions will lead into a discussion of the next section).

3. What do you think of the combination of social and educational activities as the main thrust of a centre programme for Jessie?

4. What would you suggest is the role of the field social worker in this case?

5. How would you interpret a community work function in connection with a day service? How would this operate in a situation such as Jessie's?

6. What is meant by a resource centre? Do you think this function is fulfilled in this case?

Chapter four

The ablest amongst the less able?

Many centres would acknowledge that they have some clients who could be regarded as the 'ablest amongst the less able' and who, because they are more able, can be helpful to others.

Catherine and Wendy are two examples. Both scored the maximum twenty out of twenty on the features of performance scale we used in the research for assessing performance in carrying out self-management and daily living tasks. They could look after themselves in terms of personal care and could perform normal daily living tasks. They could read and write (as it happened, both of them could type). They could do their shopping without difficulty and any disadvantages they had were, perhaps, social rather than intellectual. Catherine, for example, had tended through habit to allow her parents to do too much for her because, as a child, she had been 'slow'. Wendy had become, perhaps because of past experiences, more dependent on others than most people are when it came to going out or travelling.

The question arises: why do people like Catherine and Wendy attend adult training centres? Is it to focus on the very specific limitations they have which we have referred to? If it were so, their attendance might easily be part-time and for a limited period. Or do ATC's instead aim to offer such people a general programme of 'training', linked with opportunities to pursue social activities? If so, why? Is it really for their particular benefit? Or is there another partly hidden issue, namely, the extent to which centres depend on the ablest of their clients to help out with the others, especially when there are staff shortages or other staff limitations? If this seems a provocative or controversial statement, let us consider the evidence.

Catherine

Catherine, aged thirty, lives with her mother, father and sister. The mother does not work, but at one time she did. Looking back to that time, she commented: 'We really needed Catherine at home, but I managed to cope to allow her to attend the centre.' When I asked the mother whether she thought it would benefit her (i.e. the mother herself) that Catherine attended, she replied: 'No, she is quite capable of looking after herself.' In other words, there was no question of the mother needing respite. She acknowledged that Catherine, who had attended normal schools, was 'just slow'.

The centre places a particular emphasis on clients being able to help one another.

Catherine herself said she attended the centre to 'meet new people'. She has also learnt to do new things - for example, to type. She had learnt cooking. And now, she said, she gets 'fed up' when the centre is shut. She would, indeed, like to attend more often in the evening. According to the mother's account, it was really Catherine herself who decided she wanted to attend in the first place - after the idea had been put to her.

At the centre, the key staff person described Catherine as 'a very competent young woman'. She added: 'She takes an interest in outside activities and involves herself in what is going on at the centre.'

The network diagram, for the first monitored fortnight, is shown in *figure twelve*. First, we may note that Catherine walks to the nearest town to do her shopping. This is a distance of about three miles. There is an occasional bus service which Catherine also uses, and, when she does so, she is able to travel by herself. (This is not shown during the fortnight studied). However, when she travels to the centre in the same town, she is collected by special bus. She also uses the special bus, as the diagram shows, to travel with others out from the centre to the swimming baths.

Secondly, the punctilious way in which she has listed her activities at the centre is notable, as well as the large number of clients and staff she has named. Amongst her activities during this fortnight are typing menus for the centre cafeteria.

Here are some staff comments on some of these activities:

ACTIVITIES	OBJECTIVES and COMMENTS
Tapestry.	Accuracy to the pattern. Neatness and starting and finishing by herself. Catherine found difficulty getting into the rhythm of a single tent stitch. She could identify her mistakes and has the patience to work it out.
Typed menu.	Catherine types the menus for the centre and accuracy is required. Her typing is accurate.
Keeping diary.	Catherine is very painstaking and diary occupies quite a large part of her day.
Education - working on change - giving from 10p, 20p, 50p and a pound.	To consolidate earlier work on this skill and develop confidence in handling change.
	Catherine manages to perform these tasks with apparent ease in

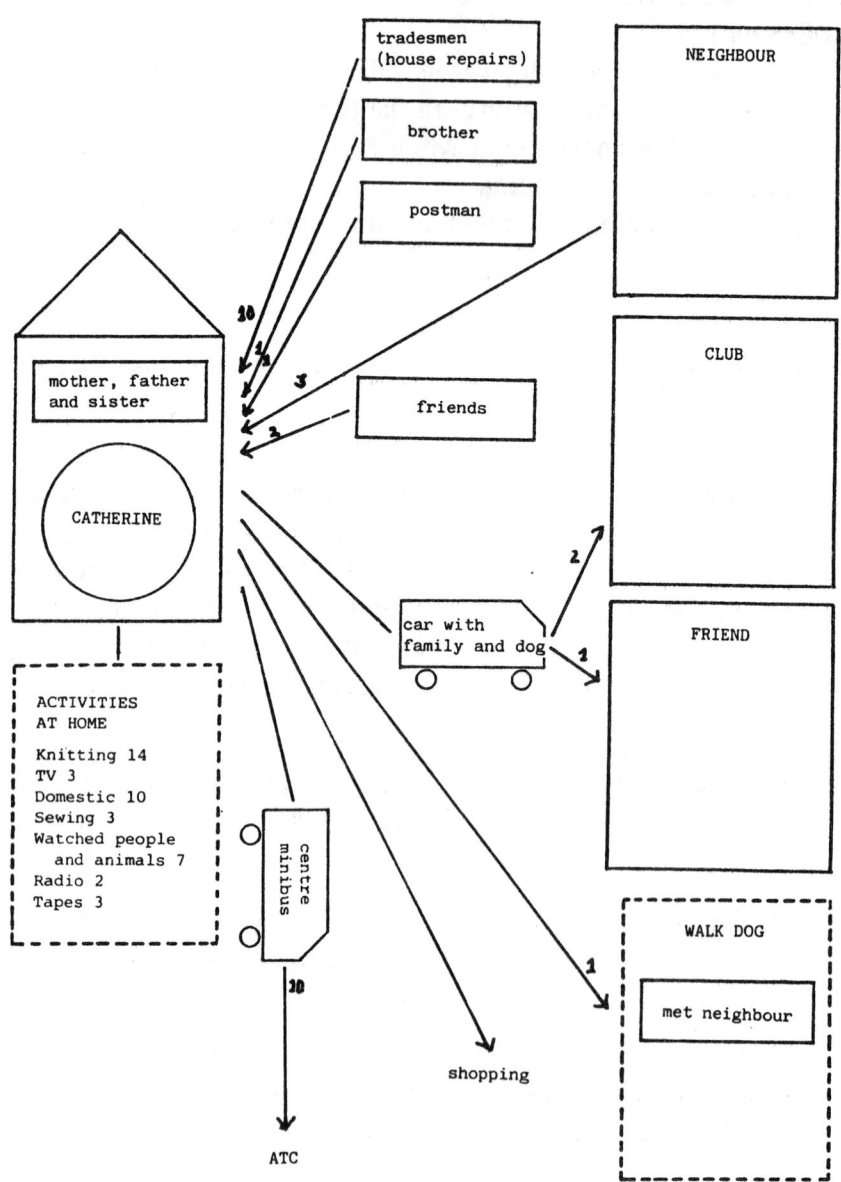

Fig. 12a - Catherine, First Monitored Fortnight (Centre-based Network)

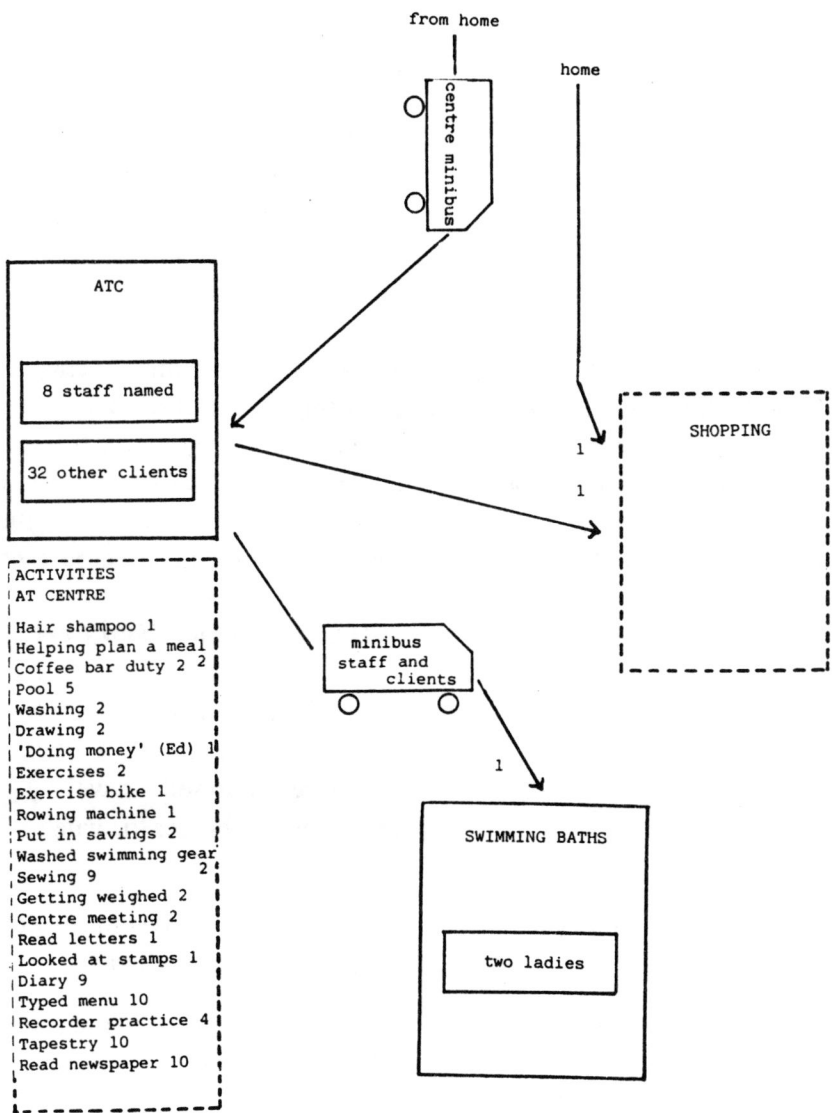

Fig. 12b - Catherine, First Monitored Fortnight (Centre-based Network)

the context of an educational session but sometimes lacks confidence when attempting to perform these same tasks in another context, e.g. when she is on duty at the centre coffee bar. As always, Catherine was cheerful and co-operative.

There was little development in Catherine's programme of activities from the first to the second monitored fortnight - with a space of a year in between. We have not illustrated the network diagram for the second monitored fortnight because she happened to be away on a family holiday. Instead, we quote below a list of activities at the centre and the staff objectives and comments for the period immediately preceding this.

ACTIVITIES	OBJECTIVES and COMMENTS
Craftwork.	To teach her new skills. To make her feel she's producing a product for the centre to sell. I have problems getting her to change her activities.
Newspaper reading.	To promote an interest in current affairs (as for other clients).
Weight awareness.	To help her be aware of foods (as for other clients).
Activities for daily living.	To give her more confidence, wider horizons, independence. 'Mum will be doing it because Catherine is away at the centre.

	Therefore Catherine is not getting the chance to do it at home. Therefore this activity at the centre is important'.
Ladies group.	To develop self-awareness. Coping with friends. Better hygiene.
Music. Recorder playing.	To achieve something which is *her* desire. To give support to do this. (A problem is that not a lot of time can be spent with each person)
Checking public transport routes.	'If *she* is in the position to travel...'
Education.	With a view to self-satisfaction, to develop her education, especially writing skills. Calculations. 'I don't know how much she'll do outside the centre. Mother does things for her.'

There appear to be no plans for Catherine to leave the centre. At this centre there was no particular emphasis on achieving 'throughput'. Catherine could expect to remain there indefinitely.

Wendy

Wendy is older than Catherine. She attended an ordinary school. After leaving school she had a number of jobs. She did not keep these jobs at a time when she was also depressed. She was referred as a day patient to the nearest hospital for adults with mental handicaps. After ten years there, she went to an adult training centre in another town for four years and then transferred to the local centre, which she now attends. This

6. Why do you think you come to the Centre?

.........TO LEARN TO LOOK AFTER YOURSELF....
....AND TO EDUCATE MYSELF BETTER.........
........TYPING

7. Is there anything you have learnt at the Centre which has helped you at home (or at the hostel etc)? What?

........TYPING

8. Is there anything you especially like doing at the Centre? What is your favourite thing?

........TYPING

9. Is there anything you would like to do at the Centre which you don't already do?

........No.

10. Would you like to go to the Centre more/less often?

........MORE OFTEN.

11. Do you like it when the Centre is shut?

........NO, BORED. EASY.

12. Would you like to do things at the Centre in the evenings? What sort of things?

........YES. BINGO MEMORY

Figure 13 - part of an interview schedule completed by Wendy

was a smaller centre and was newly opened. I was told that when the manager first saw Catherine she asked her what she would like to learn to do. She immediately replied: 'To learn to type'. She was soon given a room and a typewriter and, at the time when I met her, she was typing competently and preparing to take 'O' level examinations.

Wendy was capable of filling in her own interview schedules, which the researcher normally completes in discussion with clients. We know that the information she gave was correct although some further information was gathered in a joint interview with herself and her mother. We learnt that after leaving school, she worked for two years in a bakery. The mother insisted Wendy could do the work but wouldn't. When she was referred to the hospital, there was no other day service in the area at the time.

Wendy gave us her written views about the centre and why she attended. Part of her answers are reproduced in *figure thirteen*.

Wendy leads an active life outside the centre as we can see from the network diagram for the first monitored fortnight (*figure fourteen*). Her network includes 'normal places' but not necessarily normal people other than such contacts as shopkeepers. The centre is very important to her. She also goes there at weekends to water plants in the greenhouse. She spends a lot of time with her sister.

Although Wendy had been encouraged to learn to type, the staff view at the beginning of the research was that Wendy attended to give her an interest. It was not in the expectation she would get employment. 'Whenever an interest is expressed,' I was told, 'you try to develop it a bit further to see if there's something there that we haven't discovered yet.'

By the time of the second monitored fortnight (see *figure fifteen*), a year later, her activities appeared to be more focused on the possibility of developing activities outside the centre and, especially, in taking advantage of further education opportunities. It will be seen that amongst her centre activities were: 'type letters for manager'. (The centre does not have a secretary). She continues to visit the centre at weekends to

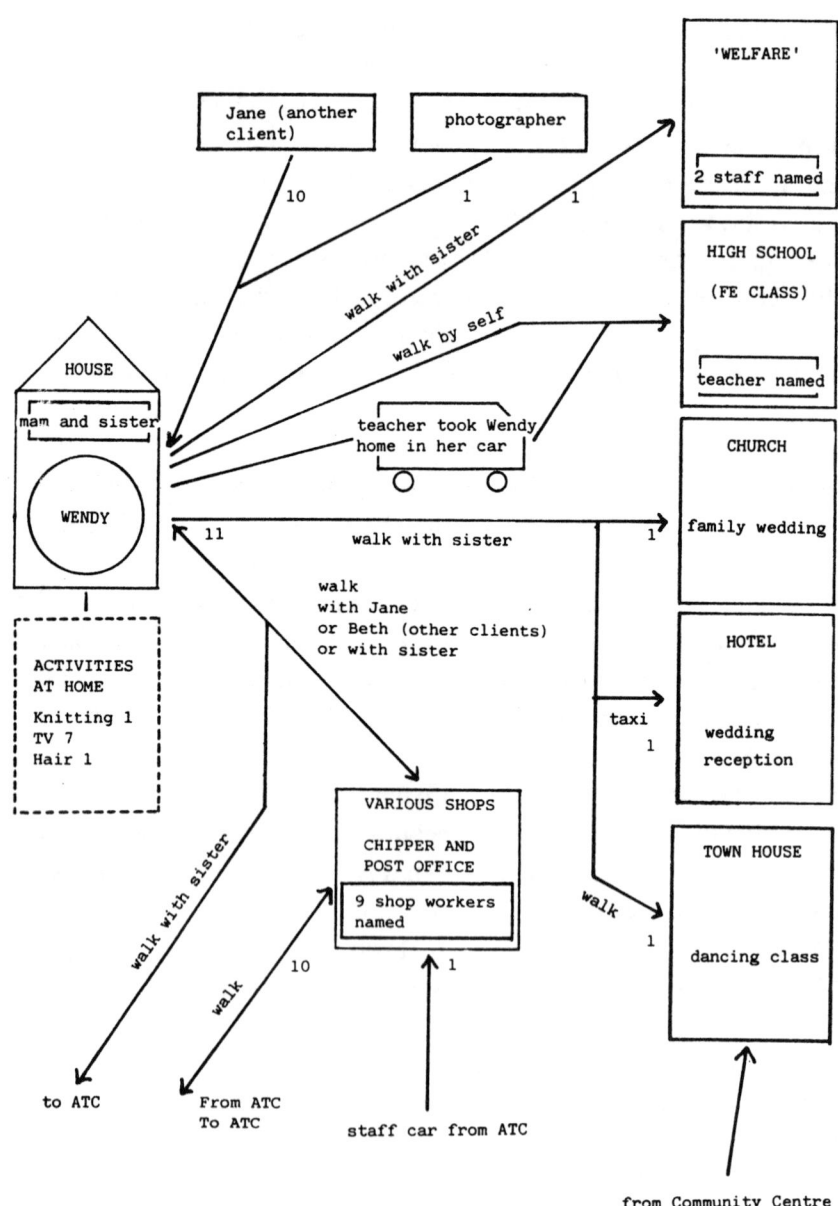

Fig. 14a - Wendy, First Monitored Fortnight (Home-based)

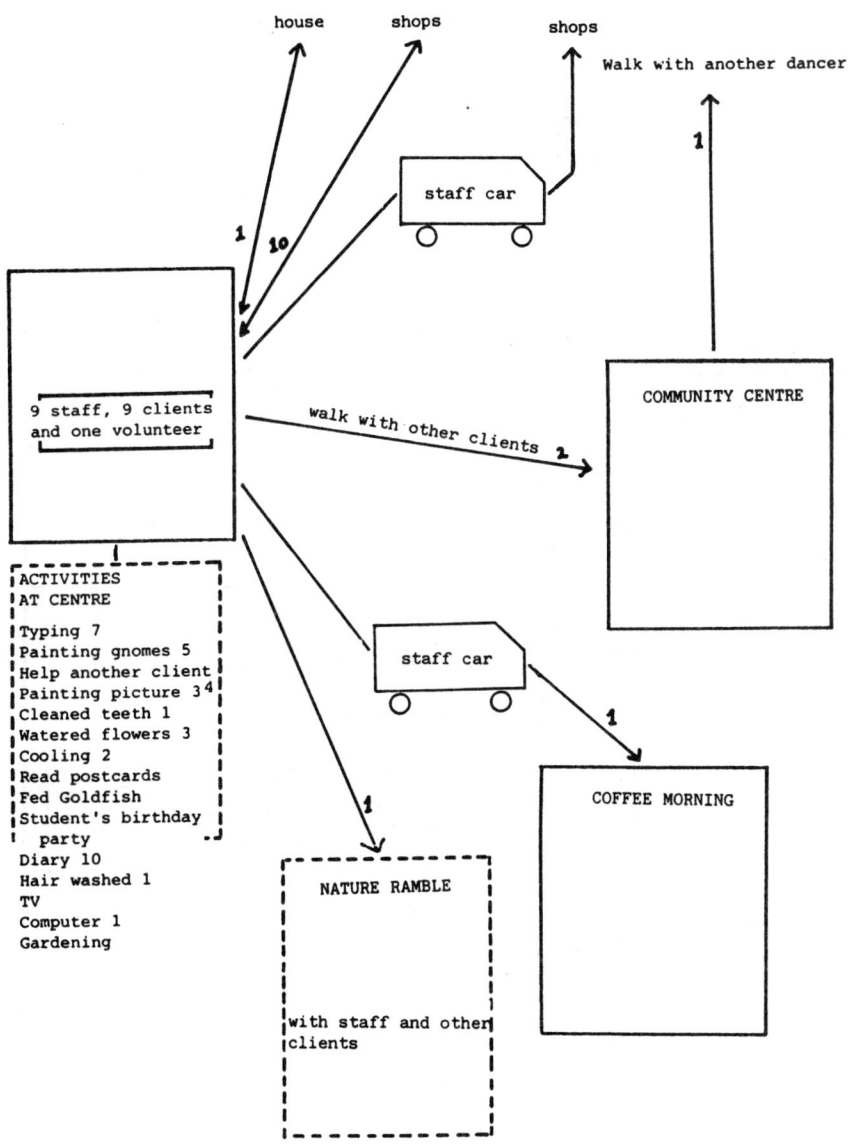

Fig. 14b - Wendy, First Monitored Fortnight (Centre-based)

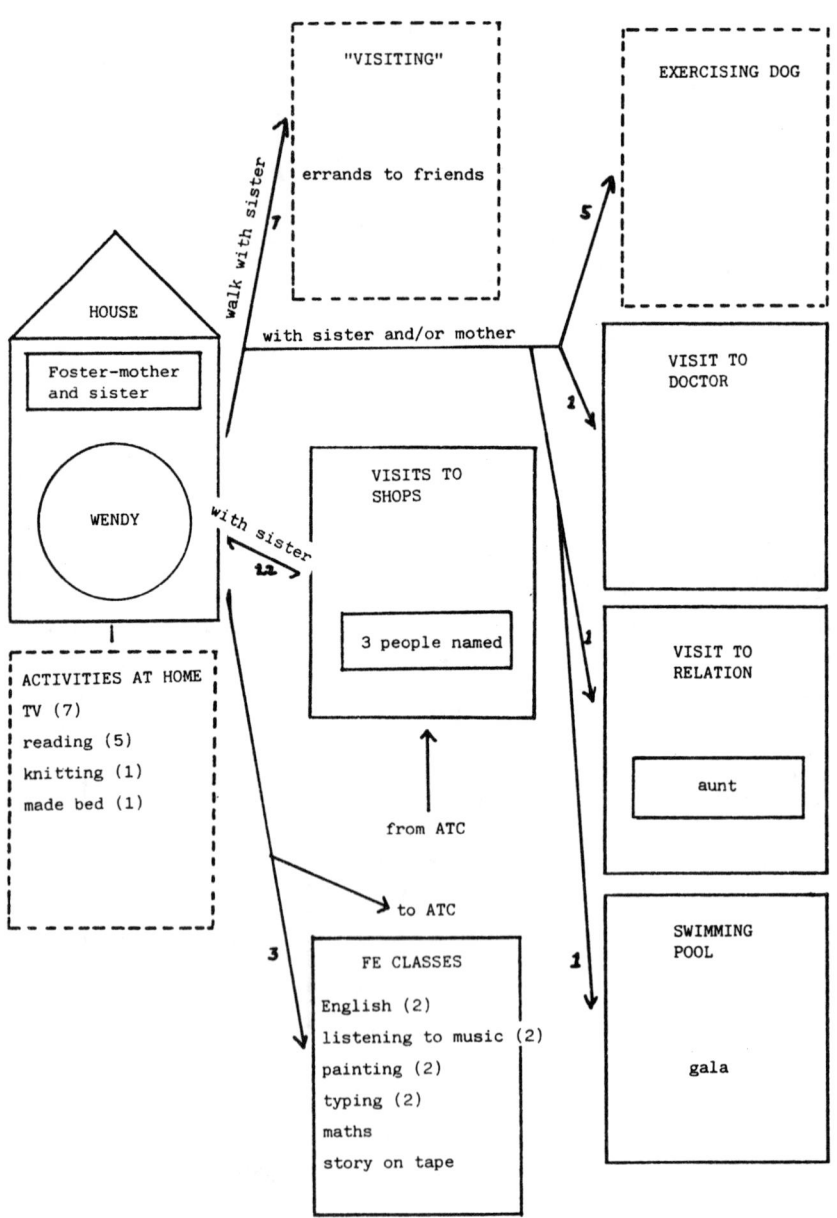

Fig. 15a - Wendy, Second Monitored Fortnight (Home-based)

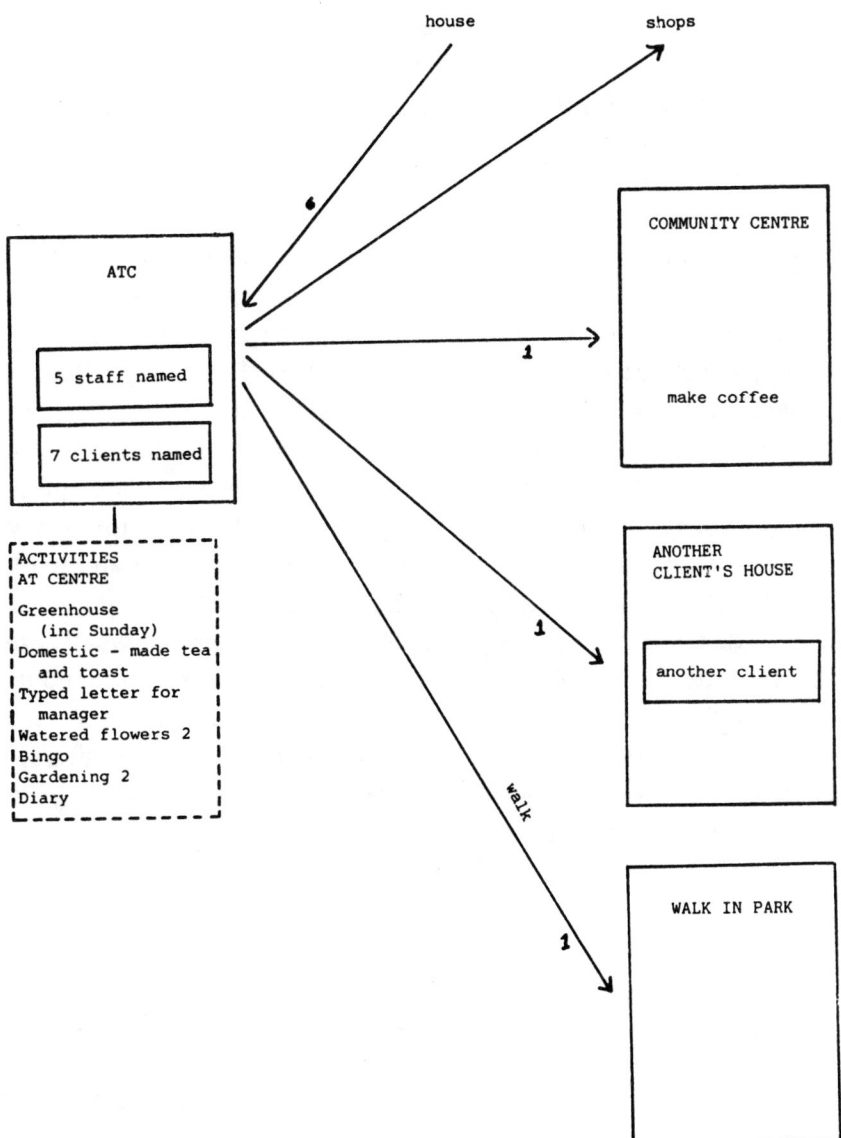

Fig. 15b - Wendy, Second Monitored Fortnight (Centre-based)

help look after the greenhouse. But more time is now spent attending further education classes and the range of activities there is now broader.

It will also be noticed from the second monitored fortnight that Wendy's many visits from home are still in company with others. She seldom travels unaccompanied.

What, then, were the activities and objectives as seen by staff for the second monitored fortnight? From a written timetable staff had prepared for one of the two weeks studied, we can see that Wendy's activities, as perceived by the staff, could be put into two categories. Firstly, some activities are intended to help Wendy learn. For example 'Maths' at the FE class. Secondly, and featuring more often, it is clear from the way the activities are described that a lot of what Wendy was intended to be doing was helping out. Even at the FE class, when doing English, she was 'asked to type a letter for the teacher.' Of course, this would help her typing. At the domestic unit, she was making tea and toast, clearing the table and washing the dishes. We know, however, she could already do these things (though her mother complained she was lazy in this respect). On the Friday, she was in the café at the community centre, where a group of clients participate. She was serving tea and rolls. It is stated that she did all the clearing up and did the washing up. Even when she was playing bingo on Friday afternoon, she was helping other clients to mark off numbers.

These are the answers staff gave when asked about the objectives for these and some other activities:

ACTIVITY	OBJECTIVES and COMMENTS
Painting.	She enjoys it, mixing with others in the community.

Typing for manager.	Enjoyment. To give her practice. She was asking for a new typewriter.
Domestic unit.	To do things for herself, because her mother is getting older.
Bingo.	Helps less able clients to mark counters. She likes to be able to help the others. Sometimes her sister comes in as well.
FE College (English, Maths, etc.)	She enjoys it. Mixing with others in the community.

Other objectives for activities during the second week of this monitored fortnight (showed in the network diagram but not in the timetable) are similar. For example, she undertakes gardening because 'she loves plants and flowers'. It was also said that she gardens at home for a neighbour. She was helping with hairdressing at the centre because she 'enjoys doing it'.

There is no doubt that Wendy thoroughly enjoys attending the centre. She is gaining in confidence, through learning to do things she has not had the opportunity to do before (e.g. typing).

Catherine and Wendy may be fairly exceptional people within their particular centres. Our research experience suggests, however, that it is not exceptional for centres to have such people attending amongst their other clients. There are usually one or two who are the 'ablest amongst the less able'.

Points for Discussion

1. Both Catherine and Wendy enjoy attending day centres. The centres form the major part of their lives outside home. They have a role to play in the centres helping others. Should they be attending ATC's

on a long-term basis? If not, what are the alternatives? What should the centres be doing to prepare them for a move? If you think they should attend long-term, is this in keeping with the service ATC's are intended to provide?

2. It might be supposed that Catherine could attend other community facilities in order to pursue some of the activities, or learn some of the things, recorded above. Yet this is in a rural area in the West of Scotland where no College of Further Education is accessible. On the other hand, she already attends a club run by a voluntary organisation which has taught her first aid. One wonders if other clubs would be available in the local town to meet other interests she has. What is your view?

3. Is there evidence that centres want to keep their ablest clients because they can be helpful to others, or because their presence is enjoyed by staff and other clients?

4. If the ablest clients are being useful in helping at centres, should this be recognised in payments they receive? If so what would be the implications for other allowances they may receive?

5. Do you think that because Catherine and Wendy are relatively able, special problems they may have could be neglected? What might these problems be? What could be done to focus on these problems and offer help?

6. Although it is now past history, can you see any justification for Wendy attending as a day patient at a long-stay hospital for people with a mental handicap? (At the time there was no local day centre available).

7. Supposing Catherine and Wendy were at their respective referral positions today, i.e. they had left ordinary schools and, perhaps, tried and failed to retain employment and (in Wendy's case) felt depressed. Would you think it right to admit them to adult training cen-

tres? If so, what would you suggest as their training programmes? If not, what would you suggest as the alternatives?

8. Do you see evidence of Catherine and Wendy being 'institution-alised' and dependent on day care? How is this dealt with in considering alternatives for the future?

9. If Catherine and Wendy were to leave their centres, what would be the implications for others they help? Would the role they had in helping others be filled by other clients? If so, is this (i) desirable or (ii) undesirable, being a substitute for employing additional staff?

10. Perhaps there is no absolute right and wrong in answering some of the questions we have posed, but it may be a question of economy. Perhaps Catherine and Wendy will learn, in the long run, to be more independent. The question then becomes, are there ways in which this goal could be achieved by more focused programmes relating to their specific learning or other needs?

Chapter five

Day services in rural areas

People living in rural areas have to travel to towns for many of the services they need - for example, major shopping, visiting the dentist, government offices. Should this apply also to day services for people with mental handicaps? Research in Scotland has revealed examples of people being bussed up to forty miles each way over mountainous roads each day to attend a day centre.

In some cases, where there are no local services, people with handicaps stay at home. For example I came across a situation very recently where a mother lived alone with her daughter who had profound and multiple handicaps and who was in her mid-thirties. They lived in a village about fifteen miles from the nearest town. They were very attached and involved with each other and spent nearly all their days in each other's company. The daughter had never been to school and was unknown to the Social Services Department. Probably even her existence was only known to a few people.

There are perhaps three ways in which the problem of delivering day services to people with handicaps has been tackled. The first is by introducing a mobile service. A proposal for a mobile resources unit was first made for the Scottish Highlands as early as 1979, but it was not taken up at that time. In the early 1980s, an experiment was launched in North Yorkshire described as 'a novel method of delivering an appropriate and viable day training service to mentally handicapped adults living in rural areas.' The idea was 'to take a service into the areas rather than transporting rurally-based clients to, or accommodating them in, towns.' A double decker bus was converted and two areas were selected for the experiment.

This service is still being provided, but instead of extending it to other areas a second kind of approach is being developed. This is the idea of very small locally-based units, with ten-twelve places each. A similar idea is being pursued in some other areas including in the situation quoted earlier where people had to bus over forty miles over the mountains.

The third approach has been to develop outreach services, in the form of a peripatetic instructor, from a town-based centre. One such scheme is described in this chapter. We shall contrast it with a second case where a complicated daily journey to a centre in a city is undertaken.

Alf

In 1984, when the researcher (Margaret Thomson) first visited the family, Alf was aged thirty-eight. His mother was in her sixties. Alf's father had recently died and other members of the family had left home. Alf and his mother were alone and each was very dependent on the other.

The mother told the researcher, when they had got to know each other, that she had been very anxious in the beginning about being 'part of the research'. Although it had been explained that this was part of a study with a random sample the mother had imagined that it might lead to Alf being taken away from her and placed in a hostel. In the long-run she recognised such a move might be necessary. Her brother had offered to take her should anything happen to the mother but the mother felt that this would not be the best solution.

Alf and his mother live in a village some thirty-five miles from the nearest day centre and about fifteen miles from the nearest social work office. There are local schools in the village. Alf attended a normal village school and went on to the local secondary school. The mother said it was made clear to her that his attendance was to give her a rest and not in the expectation that he would learn anything! The mother re-called that there was, however, one teacher who was keen to get in-volved with Alf and to teach him but a problem arose about the teacher spending so much time with him at lunch times. The mother said this was not acceptable to the school system.

Alf received no help after school until he was aged thirty-two and then a group of mothers got together with help from a social worker and started an afternoon club for adults with handicaps held in the church hall. The club is still going and Alf still attends. The club re-ceives financial help from the Local Authority Education Department and it is under the umbrella of a national parents' organisation. It is, however, independent and raises a substantial proportion of its costs by local fund raising.

Alf is fairly capable at what we call self-management skills. He is able to walk although he does not in fact go further than a visit to neigh-bours, occasionally by himself. He needs help with shaving (from mother). Physical help is needed for bathing partly because of his weight and partly because he is afraid of certain things including water. He can communicate although there are some difficulties. The mother said that Alf is sometimes 'quite clever with remarks' but 'it is difficult to get him to communicate sometimes. He gives up if you do not listen properly. He turns his head away.' Margaret Thomson herself re-corded: 'I found it quite difficult to communicate with Alf because his mother kept prompting him or answering the questions for him. His speech is reasonable, although answers come in single words or in words which take a while to decipher. Once he gets going with the con-versation, though, he can string words together quite easily and make sentences once he's got the hang of it.'

A social worker is in touch with this family visiting about every six months. Usually, according to the mother 'to give information'. Some-times, however, he does more. During one visit during the first moni-tored fortnight (see *figure sixteen*) the social worker came and transported Alf to his voluntary club. This was unusual and was on ac-

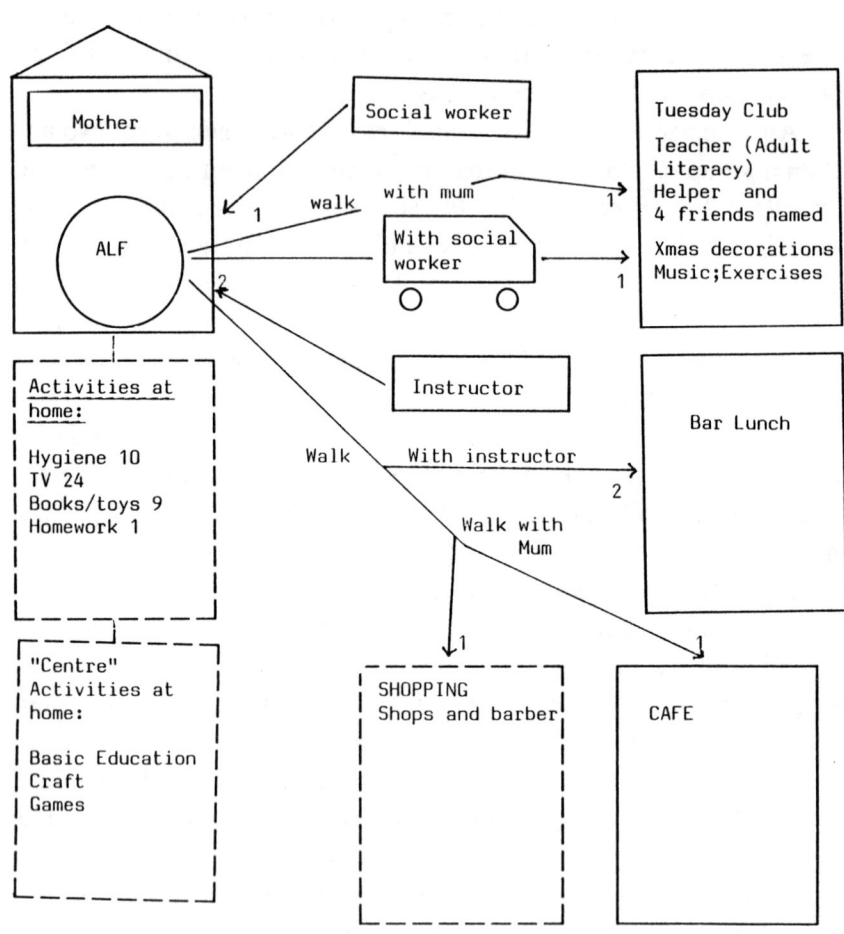

Fig. 16 - A fortnight in Alf's life, November 1984

count of the weather and because he was in the village on other business.

Alf does not attempt the journey of thirty-five miles to the nearest day centre. Instead the instructor from the day centre visits him at home on a peripatetic basis. She attends for the day from about ten o'clock in the morning until three in the afternoon and takes him out for a bar lunch. There is considerable emphasis on teaching during these visits. Some of the specific activities and comments recorded by the instructor during the first monitored fortnight (November 1984) were as follows:

ACTIVITY	COMMENTS
Writing: shape, copying.	Trying to maintain a failing skill. Slight improvement each week.
Number: recognition in grouping to ten.	
Colour: naming.	Knows only four colours consistently.
Reading: recognition of family names.	Expect improvement. Each day recognises more words.
Time: hours, half hours.	Struggling - excellent at hours but blocks out half hours.
Hand work: peg bag simple.	Can only work with constant supervision.
In and out on canvas.	One-to-one guidance but is improving. Although Alf is not

	particularly good at hand work. He likes it and is eager to produce a finished article.
Games - all educational from which great stores of information can be built up.	Alert, cheeky and amazingly knowledgeable in certain areas. We have built up information on football, music, animals and TV.
Animal lotto.	Wholehearted participation. Alf at his best. This is our usual way to end the day. Alf is the type of person who, in a crowd, would easily get overlooked but who has lots to offer when coaxed and encouraged.

The instructor explained to us that the peripatetic service to Alf was first introduced in 1982.

'After many hours spent at home with a sick father (who has since died) and an anxious mother, Alf had become "elderly" and set in his ways. As his name was on the hostel waiting list and he would hopefully be offered a place at the centre, it was felt that an effort to prepare him for this event would be beneficial to him. Bearing this in mind my programme was similar to what he would experience in the centre.'

She also commented that during the summer 'much time is spent out of doors (something Alf did not do too much of) and we have managed to lessen greatly his numerous fears, e.g. of wind, aeroplanes, dogs and noises'.

The instructor also attends the voluntary club. During the first monitored fortnight the instructor recorded that 'because of various unforeseen reasons no helper was present so I took the club today.' She recorded that Alf was quite biddable and had a pleasant nature. 'He

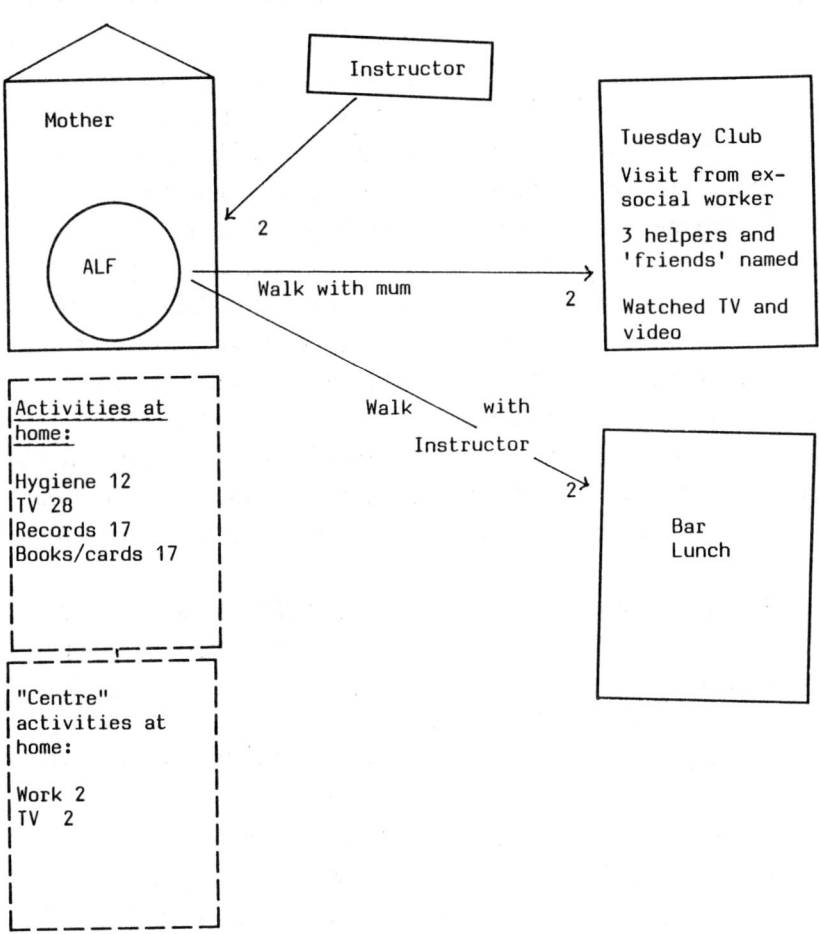

Fig. 17 - A fortnight in Alf's life, April 1986

tries well within limited ability.' During the tea break I noted that Alf's manners were excellent but that he was reluctant to help with clearing up. There was wholehearted participation during musical exercises.

The mother sees the purposes of contact with the instructor, both at the club and at home as both educational and social. She recognises that without the contacts Alf's life would be very restricted. She recognises that slow progress is also being made. The village has its own local shops and amenities. However, for major shopping it is necessary to travel thirty-five miles and the family has no car. The mother reported that it was just possible to get there and back in a day by bus.

During the second monitored fortnight, eighteen months later, (see *figure seventeen*) there was no expedition to town. The only visit out of the house was to the weekly club. On this occasion Alf met his old social worker who, some years earlier, had been partly instrumental in starting the club. This time he also met three of the voluntary helpers as well as others attending whom he describes as friends.

Daily diaries for both monitored fortnights were completed by Alf's mother. There is no real difference between the entries in 1986 and in 1984. The following are the entries for the day the past social worker came:

Got up as usual washed and dressed. Had breakfast and watched Play School on TV. This is the day I go to my club so once I have my lunch mum takes me along to the church hall where my class is held. Mum collects me at four o'clock.

(At the club) I meet my friends at the club. We all have a lovely time. Mrs ... is our teacher and Miss ... and Mrs ... help her. They are all lovely people and my friends and I are all happy.

(In the evening) After my meal about five o'clock I just do the same thing most evenings - watch TV and look at my books till bed time. We had a visit from our old welfare officer. He now works in .... We all miss him very much. He is such a nice man. It was lovely seeing him. He had a video so we saw ourselves on the TV. We all enjoyed his visit very much.

It will be seen not only that mother 'mothers' Alf but that she identifies with him very closely and it is difficult to tell whose feelings are being noted in the diary, mother's or Alf's.

In many ways Alf gives the impression of being older than his years. It almost seems as though he is moving from childhood to being elder-ly without the intervening stage of manhood. Yet mother is aware of changes for the better. At the end of the second monitored period, the mother thought that some things had been learnt. Weekly visits to the instructor had helped him to learn she said. He is learning writing. He likes the bar lunch. He would like it more often. In answer to the spe-cific question about whether anything had been learnt she said that Alf had greater confidence about going to the hostel. This is where he goes for respite periods and where a place is available for him when he and his mother agree that the time for this has come. Yet even after the sec-ond monitored fortnight in answer to the question as to whether Alf has learnt to express choices the mother replied that he did not have many opportunities.

After the second round of diaries were completed, we asked Alf to name the three most important people in his life. These were (apart from his mother) the instructor, the ex-social worker and his brother. It was interesting when we went into each of these relationships to examine their qualities, that in no instance did it appear that there was any opportunity for Alf to undertake tasks to help any of them.

The mother has had various breaks from caring for Alf. On one oc-casion she went for a stay on the continent while Alf went to his brother's house. Alf and his mother also went together for a week's stay in a different area arranged by the weekly club and held at a university. The mother said she enjoyed it and became very aware of how much she mothers Alf. At one point during the weekend, Alf was in the queue for food. The mother said that she went to take over and get his food for him when somebody told her to leave him to get on with it himself. She said this made her realise just how much she did fuss over him.

Postscript

The researcher contacted the family three years later (March 1989) in preparation for this chapter.

There was little change in the situation. Alf still attends the Tuesday Club once a week and is still very enthusiastic about this. He still sees his peripatetic instructor once a week.

There are plans to increase Alf's visits to the hostel for respite and this year it is possible that he will be there for up to four weeks (as distinct from two in previous years).

Alf goes in to the centre party at Christmas time and this year on his birthday he especially asked to go into the centre for the day. This was arranged and he enjoyed that trip.

Alf was quite ill last year with some condition that was unidentifiable. This caused a great deal of concern both for him and for his mother. He lost two stone in weight (which he has now put back on again) and was very poorly for a while. He has now fully recovered. His mum thought that she was going to lose him.

There is very little social work involvement with Alf. It is felt by the peripatetic instructor that this is not needed. If this were the case and it was felt there was a need for other support this would immediately be initiated by the instructor.

Alf's mother is still very anxious about her involvement with professionals and is really frightened that Alf may be 'taken away' if she is not doing things properly.

She has been reassured that there will be a place for Alf at the hostel in Perth when the time is right and that will be when his mother agrees that it is right. The researcher added: 'Alf's mum can be seen as similar to a number of elderly parents caring for middle-aged handicapped people. There is a mutual dependence on each other. Caring for Alf seems to be mother's motivation to keep going herself. She would be "lost" without him.'

Points for Discussion

1. Assess the value to Alf of:

   (i) the weekly club started through local initiative and with the help of a social worker and

   (ii) the peripatetic instructor from the nearest day centre.

2. Alf himself says he would like the instructor to come more often. Yet the researcher commented that Alf probably gets more attention in one day than he would get in a week were he to attend the centre full time. Discuss the benefits and cost effectiveness of:

   (i) An instructor visiting five families in the remote rural area once each day of the week and

   (ii) An instructor responsible for, say, eight students attending a day service.

3. Comment on mother's attachment to Alf. How does this affect the consideration of where Alf is going to live in the future? Should the mother be persuaded that if Alf leaves home it is not necessarily because of her inability to cope but because Alf could be encouraged to lead a life of greater independence? Do you think more active steps should be taken to encourage Alf to leave home - or do you consider that such steps should have been taken a long time ago?

4. Discuss the difficulties of transport in a rural community for someone who has no car. Although going out to the shops after a long bus journey is a major event, would there be correspondingly greater benefits from this event for Alf than if the mother had a car?

5. Comment on the role of the social worker in this case. Do social workers in rural areas have more time than their urban counterparts for such activities as escorting clients with handicaps and, in an emergency, taking over the running of a club?

6. Discuss the possible benefits Alf might have gained were he to start schooling today, instead of thirty years ago.

7. Discuss the consequences for Alf of his not having the opportunity to do things for others.

8. In general, Alf's social network at home could be described as very restricted or self-contained. Assess the value of the Tuesday Club and the peripatetic instructor's visits in enhancing Alf's social network. Do you think any further efforts could be made and if so, how, to develop Alf's social network and possibly his mother's network as well?

Michael

Michael was aged twenty-two when the researcher first contacted him. He lived with his mother and father, two younger brothers and one older brother. An older sister who had left home was married.

The family live about five miles from the nearest village in a remote part of the countryside. They occupy a tied farm cottage. They are not on the telephone. There is no public transport in the area. Michael gets about by hitching a lift or walking.

Michael attends an adult training centre in the nearest city. He reaches the centre by a combination of special bus and ordinary transport.

Michael is one of the ablest trainees attending the centre. Both at home and at the centre, for both monitoring fortnights, he scored the maximum possible for our features of performance assessment. This included both self-management and daily living tasks. Asked what he had learnt at the centre, he replied that he cooked his own meals. His mother said he had learnt to play snooker at the centre and his instructor said that hygiene had improved.

Michael had previously attended a special school in the city. We do not know how it was that he came to be placed in a special school or why he was considered backward. Certainly there were some social

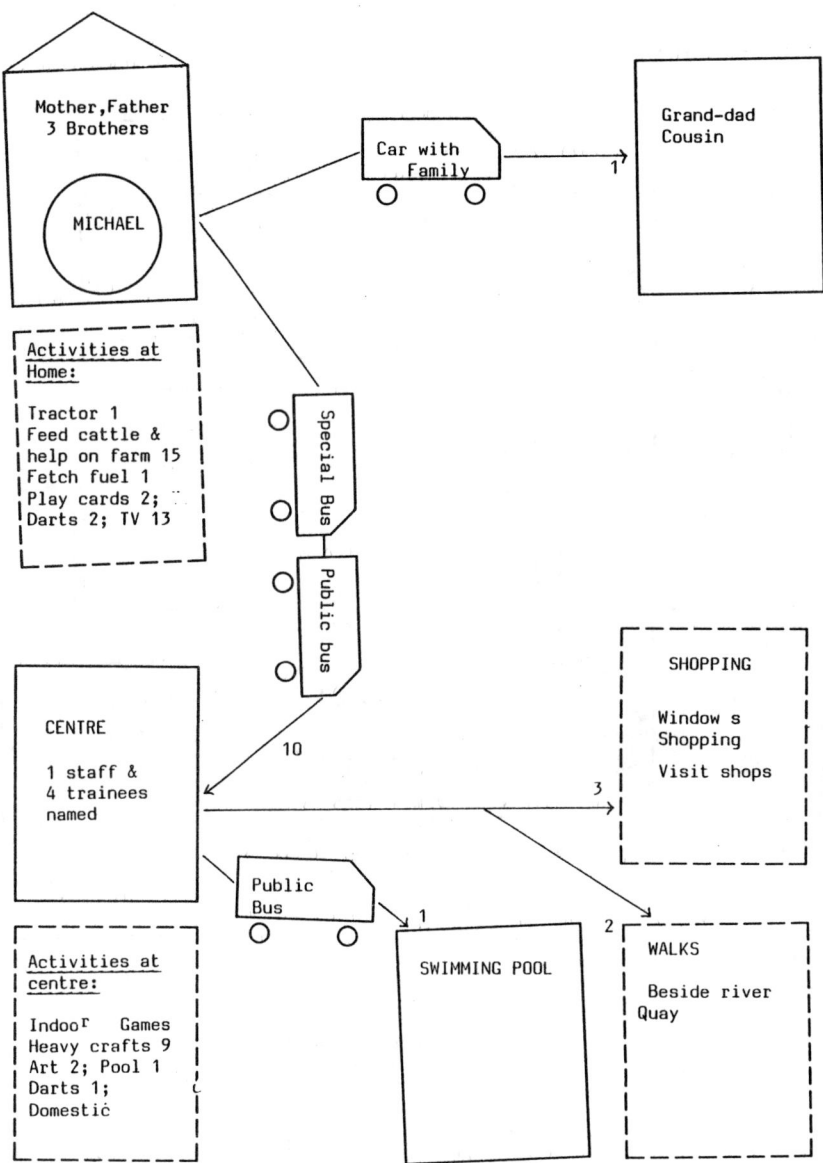

Fig. 18 - A fortnight in Michael's life, November 1984

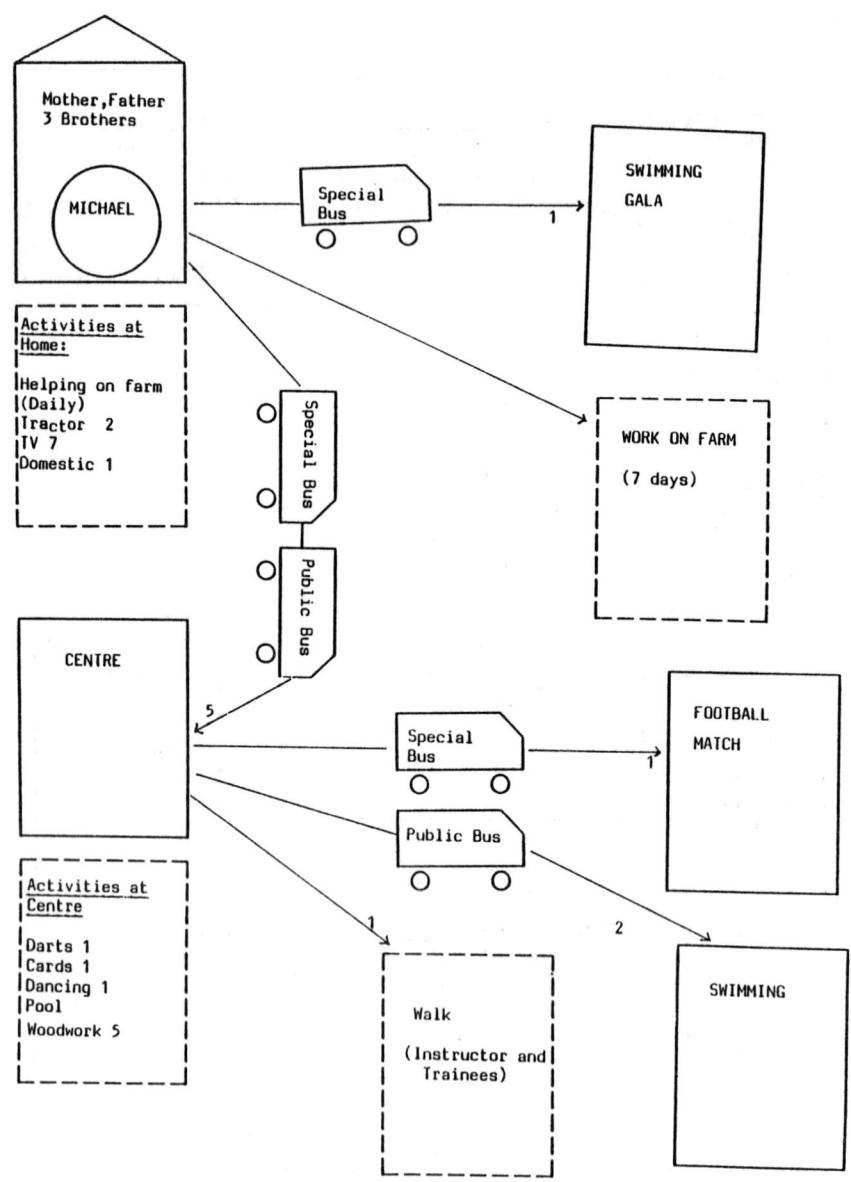

Fig. 19 - A fortnight in Michael's life, May 1986

problems. The mother said he was shy when he was younger but other children in the family were in trouble. There were reports of past incidents of fighting and regular social work visits took place because of supervision requirements.

The father is a farm labourer and mother does housework "at the big house" as required. Michael's brothers are unemployed but Michael himself helps on the farm for payment on a seasonal basis. His ambition is to work full time on a farm as proper employment.

Meantime he attends the centre. The mother is pleased about this. She heard about the centre from the special school. In answer to the researcher's question about what the mother thought he would get out of the centre she replied 'to get out more'. Asked what the mother herself would get out of it she replied "to stop worrying about finding him something to do". She said the centre did well for Michael. He likes it and they are good to him. He has lots of friends there.

The centre in question has a particular emphasis on sporting and recreational activities and Michael excels in these. His network for the first monitored fortnight in 1984 is shown in *figure eighteen*. Diaries were kept at this time with Michael by the mother at home and with an instructor at the centre. The theme in his home diary is the help he gives to others. For example:

Gave his dad a hand to tow tractor.

Gave his dad a hand to feed cattle.

Gave his dad a hand while waiting on bus.

Gave the bus driver a hand with the old people.

Gave dad a hand again.

Sorted my dad's cattle for him.

Apart from these kinds of entries, his main activity is watching the television. He goes with his mother on one occasion to visit a grand-dad and cousin but otherwise his whole social life outside the family derives from his attendance at the centre. It will be seen (*figure eighteen*) that his network from the centre is greater than his network from home and that the centre fulfils a compensatory social function.

The following are some of the entries for his activities at the centre for the same period together with staff entries for the activities he was engaged in:

Michael's Diary Kept At The Centre	Staff Diary Entries
Worked in heavy crafts making dressing table stool. At 11.45 am went to the swimming baths. Arrived back at centre 1.15 pm. Fifteen minute lunch break (mince and potato). Went for a walk to the shops in ... then played indoor games.	Woodwork till 11.30 am - making stool. Aim: to do a reasonable job. His behaviour is good and he tries to do a good job on any task given. He was then taken to the swimming baths. Aim: to swim at least one full length without a stop. In the afternoon he went window shopping. Aim: to stay together as a group and to remember some of the articles he saw when we get back to the centre. He was good all round.

For most days, entries at the centre are very similar. On one occasion, however, he was to set the table for morning tea and undertake other domestic tasks. Once he worked on an art project. Beside one activity the instructor commented: 'He can count money and write his name.' There was no record of an attempt to teach him to write more.

Diaries were kept again, about eighteen months later. (See *figure nineteen*) During this time he only attended the centre for one week, the other week (and weekend) being spent working on the farm. It will be seen that the only journey out from home, apart from the centre was to a swimming gala - and this was an event arranged through the centre. For social activities he continues to rely heavily on the centre.

It will be noticed that most of Michael's activities (apart from woodwork) during the second monitored fortnight (*figure nineteen*) involves sport or recreation. The researcher asked the instructors concerned for a statement about the objectives of each activity and comments upon any problems. These are shown below:

ACTIVITY	OBJECTIVES	COMMENTS
Football.	Competition. He enjoys it. Exercise.	There is no place to practice near to the centre so we have to travel.
TV.	Something to do.	He enjoys it.
Darts.	To improve his skills. Basic education with number counting.	Enjoys it.
Pool.	Competitiveness.	Enjoyment.
Woodwork.	To improve skills. To improve co-ordination. Work skills experience.	The group is too big.

Postscript

The researcher was not able to re-visit the family in this case, but Michael was seen at the centre (February 1989)

Michael is back in the centre having been out for a year on an open employment scheme. It was an MSC scheme and unfortunately the place where Michael was working closed down at the end of a year. There are plans to try to find him alternative employment. The instructor pointed out that Michael's parents, despite the fact that they are not well off, were very open to him having a job. This was in contrast to some of the more affluent parents of trainees in the centre who were reluctant to allow the trainees to take open employment because this greatly affected their benefits.

Points for Discussion

1. Michael appears to be 'minimally mentally handicapped'. What are the long-term effects of his having attended a special school for children with learning difficulties?

2. Granted that Michael attended a special school, should he, as a matter of course, have been offered a place at an adult training centre? What would be the alternatives today? (In answering this, bear in mind that we are talking about a rural situation).

3. Farm work is not easily available yet this is what Michael wants to do. How feasible would it have been for Michael to have left home to seek a job elsewhere, or farm training elsewhere, if these were not available locally?

4. This family has had regular attentions from a social worker. But the social worker appears to have been concerned with supervision requirements. Is there any argument for a social worker in a family like this having a wider role? How would this conflict with the prioritisation of the social worker's tasks?

5. Michael is clearly interested in sport and sporting opportunities are available through the centre. Discuss the benefits and possible limitations of this emphasis.

6. Michael goes out shopping from the centre within the city where the centre is situated. Is this likely to be helpful to Michael:

(a) in the short run?

(b) in the longer term?

7. Do you think Michael would have benefited from the kind of peripatetic services one day a week which was available to Alf?

8. Comment on the problems that can arise if employment prospects compete with the family's eligibility for welfare benefits.

Appendix

Key to network diagrams

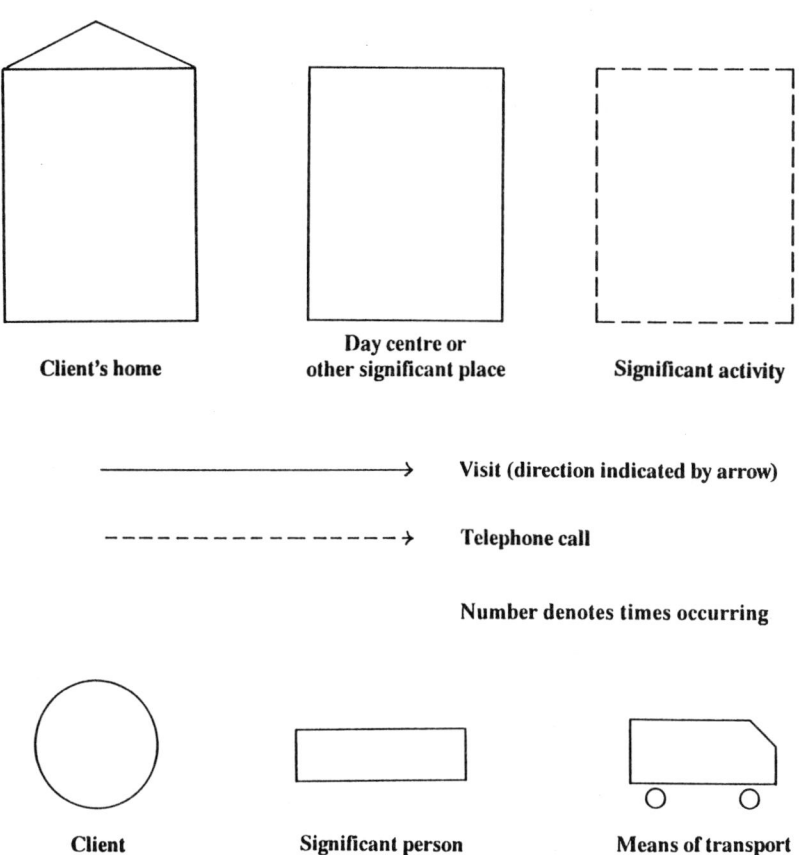

Client's home

Day centre or
other significant place

Significant activity

Visit (direction indicated by arrow)

Telephone call

Number denotes times occurring

Client

Significant person

Means of transport

Case Studies for Practice

Edited by Philip Seed

The series draws together case material from social research to illuminate and explore vital issues in social work policy and practice. Each volume in the series focuses on valuable material which has been collected in the course of research, especially research into social networks.

Philip Seed *is Senior Research Fellow at the University of Dundee. Prior to this he was Research Fellow and Honorary Senior Lecturer in the Department of Social Work, University of Aberdeen. He is the author of and contributor to many books, articles and research reports.*

Consultants: **Mike King** *(Social Care Association and Lecturer in Social Work).* **Fiona Pilkington** *(Teacher and ex-Researcher).* **Margaret Thomson** *(Researcher, Children's Panel Member, representative for the Rowntree Family Fund and member of Inverness Committee, L'Arche).* **David Mitchell** *(Social Work Education Adviser, Central Council for Education & Training in Social Work, Edinburgh Office).* **Ruth Smith** *(British Association of Social Workers).*

Social Work in the Wake of Disasters
Compiled by David Tumelty and edited by Philip Seed
1990 ISBN 1 85302 060 5

Case Studies for Practice 6
A social network approach is taken to the response of social work to disasters. The aftermath of the Piper Alpha disaster is given particular attention.

Victims of Confusion: Case Studies of Elderly Sufferers from Confusion and Dementia
Alyson Leslie
1990 ISBN 1 85302 040 0

Case Studies for Practice 5
The author describes the experiences of a number of elderly sufferers and their carers and considers to what extent their care careers were influenced by the method, timing and source of their referral for service and by the role of the agency to which they were referred.

Respite - A Social Network Approach
Edited by Philip Seed
1990 ISBN 1 85302 061 3

Case Studies for Practice 7
The case studies in this book examine the role of respite in relation to several different client groups.

HIV and AIDS - A Social Network Approach
Compiled by Roger Gaitley and edited by Philip Seed
1989 ISBN 1 85302 025 7
128 pages 210 x 145

Case Studies for Practice 4
This book examines how professionals can best care for people whose status as HIV antibody positive touches on so many of society's fears and taboos. It draws on recent case material to explore the lives of people affected directly or indirectly by HIV and AIDS. By taking account of the people, activities and environments in his or her life, a total picture emerges of where a person finds key supports - their social, legal, health and interpersonal networks, where they

complement, overlap and conflict - and illuminates the effects of any progression of the infection.

Day Services for People with Severe Handicaps
Compiled by Philip Seed
1988 ISBN 1 85302 013 3
128 pages 210 x 145
Case Studies for Practice 2
The second book in the series focuses on people with severe handicaps. The word 'severe' is used to include those who might be described in technical terms as having 'profound' or 'multiple' handicaps. In practical terms it is taken to mean people unable to perform most self-management or basic daily living tasks without substantial assistance.
CONTENTS 1. Introduction. 2. Contrasting patterns of living for two teenagers with multiple handicaps. 3. Does attendance at a centre promote a better quality of life at home? 4. Respite for carers and progress for clients - is there a conflict? 5. Patterns of living at a hostel, at home and at a day centre. 6. Physically fit but with a severe mental handicap - do centres know what to do? 7. Suggestions for further reading. Appendix - key to network diagrams.

Towards Independent Living:
Issues for Different Client Groups
Compiled by Philip Seed
1989 ISBN 1 85302 018 4
128 pages 210 x 145
Case Studies for Practice 3
There is an important social dimension to preparation for independent living. It is not just about learning how to open a tin of beans. In essence it is about social relationships and developing a better quality of life through social relationships. Clients should be enabled to be appropriately dependent on others and to allow others to be appropriately dependent on them. This book explores the ways in which this can be brought about.

The first chapter considers the outcomes for a group of young people who had a history of residential child care, followed by experience in a hostel specifically intended to enable them to live 'more independently' in the community. The next chapters consider adults with special needs: first, epileptic adults during and after in-

tensive training in a hostel, and second, a group of people who had attended an adult training centre on a part-time basis. Next there is a study of the benefits that adults who have been mentally ill can gain in learning to cope independently in society from attending a voluntary-run club at a day centre. Finally, 'independent living' is looked at in connection with the care of elderly people.

CONTENTS 1. Introduction - what do we mean by independent living? 2. Assisting young people to live independently. 3. People with mental health problems attending a day centre. 4. People with epilepsy preparing to leave a hostel. 5. A part-time day service for adults with mental handicaps. 6. Promoting independent living in residential care for the elderly. Suggestions for further reading. Key to network diagrams.

of related interest

Introducing Network Analysis in Social Work
Philip Seed
1989 ISBN 1 85302 024 9
This new textbook is designed for social workers and others in social work practice as a guide to the application of a systematic method for understanding and using social networks. As the importance of informal as well as formal care is more widely recognised, social workers and others in the helping professions have come to see the services they provide more and more in the context of the people, places and activities that are significant to the client's daily life.

In part one, social network analysis is studied generally; part two deals with specific applications of network analysis. Finally, the role of day care is studied, and procedures suggested for routine reviews using social network analysis.
CONTENTS 1. Introduction. PART 1: GENERAL. 2. What are social networks? 3. What do we mean by analysis? 4. Techniques. PART 2: SPECIFIC APPLICATIONS. 5. Fieldwork assessments. 6. Assessments prior to discharge from a residential establishment and follow-up review. 7. People leaving long-stay hospitals. 8. Day care. 9. Regular reviews. 10. Conclusion - the future. 11. Appendices.

Research Highlights in Social Work

This topical series of books examines areas currently of particular interest to those in social and community work and related fields. Each book draws together a collection of articles on different aspects of the subject under discussion - highlighting relevant research and drawing out implications for policy and practice. The project is under the general direction of Professor Gerard Rochford.

No. 17 Child Care: Monitoring Practice
Edited by Isobel Freeman and Stuart Montgomery
ISBN 1 85392 005 2 Hardback

No. 18 Privatisation
Edited by Richard Parry
ISBN 1 85302 015 X Hardback

No. 19 Social Work and Health Care
Edited by Rex Taylor and Jill Ford
ISBN 1 85302 016 8 Hardback

No. 20 Performance Review In Social Work Agencies
Edited by John Tibbitt and David May
ISBN 1 85302 017 6 Hardback

No. 21 Social Work and Disability
ISBN 1 85302 042 7 Hardback

No. 22 Social Work Response to Poverty and Deprivation
ISBN 1 85302 043 5 Hardback

No. 23 Social Work and the EC

other titles of related interest

Social Work Management and Practice:
Systems Principles
Sue Ross and Andy Bilson
1989 ISBN 1 85302 022 2 160 pages 216 x 135
The authors suggest that in many cases social work is not only ineffective but that, in the attempt to solve problems of inequality and poverty, it succeeds only in worsening the lot of those it seeks to help. Drawing on the ideas of Gregory Bateson this book applies principles drawn from his writing to the practice and management of social work. The lessons to be learnt from a writer who played a major part in the development and promotion of ideas of ecology are challenging and provide a sound theoretical

base for creative social work practice, a base which the authors show to be manifestly lacking in current practice. The authors outline principles for an 'ecology' of social work practice which recognise the importance of working with and understanding the context in which social work problems occur. They conclude that many of the assumptions underlying social work practice have to change, and propose changes not only in policy, resources and practice but also in the ideas, theories and language we use to describe them. As well as suggesting principles to guide the actions of managers and practitioners, this practical book gives many useful case examples and three longer case studies of the application of systems ideas.

Psychogeriatrics:
A Practical Handbook
Donald A. Wasylenki, Barry A. Martin, Deborah M. Clark, E. Anne Lennox, Lynda A. Perry, Mary K. Harrison,
1989 ISBN 1 85302 037 0 230 pages 235 x 155
A practical guide for all professionals who treat mental health problems in the elderly, this comprehensive handbook covers the wide range of problems encountered daily in clinical practice. It provides the means to draw the distinction between normal ageing and pathology, and applies this to clinical assessment, diagnosis and management of patients. The book contains many helpful diagrams and checklists, as well as a full index.

Psychosocial Interventions with Physically Disabled Persons
edited by Bruce W Heller, PhD, Louis M Flohr, Leonard S Zegans,
Jan 1990 246 pages 240 x 155
ISBN 1 85302 050 8 hb ISBN 1 85302 051 6 pa
This volume offers theoretical, research-based, and clinical information useful for professionals in rehabilitation, nursing, mental health, and medicine, who, in partnership with disabled persons and their families, compose the treatment/rehabilitation team. Each chapter is written by an expert in the field, most of whom are pioneers in their respective specialities.
The first section of the book includes an overview of the 'mind-body' problem as it relates to disability and a discussion of parental reactions

to the uncertainty which accompanies the birth of a seriously-impaired child. Chapters in the second section address issues in the psychological, social, and neurological evaluation of persons who are disabled. Given the impossibility of including a discussion of every disability, the third section employs four major syndromes as paradigmatic of issues encountered in four different types of disabilities. In addition, one chapter addresses the important, compelling, but often neglected area of facial disfigurement. The final section offers perspectives on independent living, psychosocial aspects of assistive devices, forensic psychiatric issues, sexuality and disability, and ethical aspects of disability. CONTENTS Preface. Part I - Background and Family Issues. Part II - Assessment. Part III - Treatment/Rehabilitation. Part IV - Social Psychological Issues. Index.

Violence Against Social Workers
Dan Norris
With a foreword by Harriet Harman MP
1990 ISBN 1 85302 041 9 216 x 135
Five social workers have been murdered by their clients since 1983. In this new book, Dan Norris discusses the explanations for, the incidence of and the nature of violence against social workers. The attitudes of social workers themselves are examined in the results of a specially conducted survey. *Violence against Social Workers* looks at the effect of how social workers work, their attitudes to clients, the problems cause by poor or undirected management and insufficient resources and information, and the legal responsiblities of management. Finally, the author explores in detail methods of controlling and reducing violence and the implications which such approaches may have for social work. in the future.

The Science and Practice of Gerontology: A Multidisciplinary Approach
Nancy J. Osgood and Ann H.L. Sontz
1989 ISBN 1 85302 044 3
The Science and Practice of Gerontology is a reference work for the variety of professionals now engaged in research and practice with the elderly. The collection of articles by experts in each area offers established scholars and practitioners, a wealth of information regarding the discipline of gerontology and the relationship of gerontology to geriatrics. The reader will find articles on the psychological, social and cultural domains affecting older people, but also those containing general biomedical understandings and practical/clinical applications.

'Share the Care': An Evaluation of a Family-Based Respite Care Service
Kirsten Stalker
1990 ISBN 1 85302 038 9
The provision of respite care within families is a relatively new development and the *ad hoc* nature of individual schemes has resulted in a great variation in their character; relatively little research has been carried out into the policy and practice of this important development in community care. *'Share the Care'* examines: the different ways in which respite care schemes operate, focusing in particular on the Share-the-Care service in Lothian; the experience of parents of children with learning difficulties of the scheme; respite carers: who joins the scheme and why, their perceptions of its rewards and dissatisfactions, and their experience of social work support; the less positive effects of separation upon the children themselves; families facing an extended wait for respite; families who withdraw from the scheme.

Dyslexia: How would I cope?
Michael Ryden
1989 ISBN 1 85302 026 5
This book draws on the experiences of several people with dyslexia, including the author himself. It is intended to increase awareness of the experience of individuals with dyslexia and to reinforce positive attitudes towards dyslexics in parents, teachers and employers: to give them the necessary knowledge of how a dyslexic is affected, and how to concentrate on their strong points in order to minimize the effects of dyslexia, and find a form of communication that is accessible to everyone concerned. Suggestions and hints are given on how best to use the dyslexic's abilities to by-pass inabilities and enable him or her to live a normal life in society.

Counselling Adult Survivors of Child Sexual Abuse

Christiane Sanderson

1990 ISBN 1 85302 045 1

The author discusses first the different theories of child sexual abuse. Part Two explores the process of uncovering the abuse, different kinds of treatment, the recurring topics which arise in treatment, and the role of the counsellor, including the effects of his or her own attitudes to abuse. Part Three broadens the focus to look at the outcomes of treatment and the role of partners and support networks. There is a bibliography and a list of organisations.

Drama and Healing: The Roots of Drama Therapy

Roger Grainger

1989 ISBN 1 85302 0486 144 pages

In Part One, the author investigates the therapeutic origins of theatre before moving on to the part played by drama in psychological maturation, leading to a discussion of depression, thought disorder and schizophrenia and the role of drama therapy in their treatment. Part Two examines the drama therapy experience and the ways in which the therapeutic possibilities of drama can be harnessed, both in improvised dramatic episodes and in theatre games, to achieve a wide range of therapeutic goals.
CONTENTS: Introduction. Part 1. Roots. 1. Drama as Involvement. 2. The Healing Symbol. 3. Drama and Depression. 4. Drama and Schizophrenia. Part 2. Process. 5. Approaches to Dramatherapy. 6. Some of the Cast. 7. Capturing the Image. 8. Healing and Truth. Appendix 1. The Use of Drama Therapy in the Treatment of Thought Disorder. Appendix 2. Instructions for Administering the Grid Test of Thought Disorder. BibliographyAdvance Title Information

Art Therapy and Dramatherapy: Their Relation and Practice

Sue Jennings and Ase Minde

1989 ISBN 1 85302 027 3 176 pages, illustrated

This is the first book to explore the relationship and differences between art therapy and dramatherapy. It is based on eight years of research and practice of art therapy and dramatherapy, in training, clinical practice and theory.

CONTENTS 1. Philosophy. 2. Art Therapy. 3. Dramatherapy. 4. The Creative and Imaginative Processes. 5. The Art Therapist and the Drama Therapist. 6. The Body. 7. Masks and Myth. 8. Transitionary Object. 9. Opening and Closing the Door. 10. The Journey. 11. Bibliography.

Dramatherapy with Families and Groups: A Handbook for Social Workers and Therapists

Sue Jennings

1989 ISBN 1 85302 014 1 160 pages

The author presents a working framework for dramatherapists, social workers, family and marital therapists, and others running groups. It deals primarily with dramatherapy in the non-clinical setting such as family centres, residential children's homes, social services resources and intermediate treatment centres. Separate chapters cover current theory, methodology and application in specific client areas including child abuse. The book addresses work with children and adults, both individually and in groups, illustrated by case history examples.

Christian Symbols, Ancient Roots

Sue Jennings and Elizabeth Rees

1990 1 85302 046 X 160 pages, illus.

This book selects dominant Christian symbols and places them against the archaic background from which they grew, drawing on myths and rituals of both ancient and contemporary cultures. It is written with a wide readership in mind: pastors, counsellors and psychotherapists, artists and anthropologists, and anyone interested in exploring the ever-present world of symbol.

The Division in British Medicine: A History of the Separation of General Practice from Hospital Care 1911-1968

Frank Honigsbaum

Preface by Professor Brian Abel-Smith

1979 220 pages 234 x 156

ISBN 0 85038 133 9 cl ISBN 0 85038 219 X pa

"... first class ... will be the definitive text on the period for many years to come." - *Medical Digest*